TRAITORS' END

NATHANIEL WEYL

TRAITORS' END

The Rise and Fall of the Communist

Movement in Southern Africa

ARLINGTON HOUSE   *New Rochelle, N. Y.*

Second Printing, October 1970

Library of Congress Catalog Card Number 71-101960

SBN 87000-082-9

MANUFACTURED IN THE UNITED STATES OF AMERICA

NOT ALL OF THE PERSONS WHOSE ACTIVITIES ARE DISCUSSED in this book are traitors. Some appear in its pages because their thoughts and activities are part of the story of the struggle of White South Africa for its continued existence; others were implicated in the subversive movement, but did not commit treasonable acts; still others could not have been traitors to South Africa, Rhodesia or Portugal because they were not citizens of any of these countries and hence owed them no allegiance.

11515

Contents

⬦ ⬦ ⬦ ⬦ ⬦

Introduction

❖ ❖ ❖ ❖ ❖

SOUTH AFRICA HAS THE PERHAPS UNIQUE DISTINCTION OF having shattered a powerful Communist movement and destroyed its political influence without abandoning parliamentary government, due process of law, or the independence and vigilance of its judiciary.

During the 1950's and early 1960's, the South African Communist Party, operating through a variety of front organizations of which the African National Congress was the most important, enjoyed wide support among the Bantu, Coloured, and Indian populations, and among White South African liberals and professionals as well. Its thrust for power, presented to the world as a movement against Apartheid, received moral support from the Soviet Union, the Afro-Asian bloc and the Kennedy Administration. South Africa, together with Rhodesia and the Portuguese possessions of Angola and Mozambique, at times seemed to be tottering under the combined blows of subversion from within and threatened invasion from without.

Throughout the 1960's, the cacophony of insult from the United Nations continued. In an effort to convince the new non-White nations of Africa and Asia that it could outbid the Soviet bloc in denouncing colonialism, imperialism and White rule, the Kennedy and Johnson Administrations supported virtually every assault on the White states of Southern Africa by their Black neighbors. At the same time, they deliberately blinded themselves to violations of the United Nations Charter by Tanzania and other Negro republics that were openly engaged in arming and training terrorists to spread murder and havoc throughout South Africa, Rhodesia and the Portuguese possessions.

Perhaps the high-water mark of this policy was the declaration by Ambassador to the United Nations Adlai E. Stevenson on March 16, 1961, that the United States would support a Russian resolution for "immediate steps . . . to transfer all power to the peoples" of Africa. This *volte face* in American policy occurred exactly one day after Communist-led Angolan Blacks had infiltrated across the Congo frontier and gone on a sadistic rampage in which Angolese men, women and children—more of them Black than White—were seized and, while alive, split lengthwise by buzz saws. Stevenson's demand that America's NATO ally, Portugal, be stripped of her African possessions was, he explained, a move that had the explicit approval of President John F. Kennedy.

The distinguished Washington correspondent of the *New York Times*, Arthur Krock, called this resolution "totally irresponsible and an incitement to more violence," excoriated the Kennedy Administration for denying Portugal the right to use force to restore order in her territories and branded Stevenson's refusal to condemn the Communist-led Negro invasion force for its butcheries as intellectually dishonest. Krock noted that, in treating her Portuguese ally in this fashion, the United States was transforming NATO into "a broken shield."

The blows against South Africa, Rhodesia and Portugal from the United States, Britain and the Soviet Union continued throughout the remainder of the Kennedy-Johnson era. Fortunately for the fate of the African continent, however, the internal situation within these beleaguered lands was being decisively transformed so as to deny the

Communists opportunity to use their international support to seize power.

Between 1948 and 1965, the Communist movement in South Africa and Rhodesia was pulverized. The South African Communist Party was reduced by 1965 to a minuscule movement, harried by the police, alienated from the Bantu, Coloured and Indian masses, despised by an overwhelming majority of the Whites and compelled to take such extreme measures of conspiratorial defense against annihilation that it lost its power to take effective political action.

The destruction of this subversive movement was the result of a combined assault, in which repression and indoctrination were the two major weapons. Stern laws were enacted, which outlawed subversive movements and punished sabotage and revolutionary attempts against the state with drastic penalties. The efficient South African National Police successfully infiltrated the Communist Party and kept it under surveillance. Believing the Communist movement to be a constant threat to due process, law and order, free institutions and the existence of the nation, South Africa arrested, prosecuted, convicted, imprisoned or drove into flight and exile Communism's leaders and seasoned cadres.

The ideological struggle against Communism was an uncompromising one. South Africa, Rhodesia and Portugal took the position that they were not dealing with a reform movement, but with forces dedicated to the destruction of stable government in Africa and throughout the non-Communist world.

Anti-Communist indoctrination was probably successful for three reasons. The first is that it was combined with repressive measures that isolated, scattered, imprisoned or destroyed the seasoned and diehard Communist militants and in the process scared off the vacillating masses of fellow travelers and parlor radicals. The halfhearted, who had joined the movement because of restlessness, curiosity, personal resentment, vague discontents, a befuddled desire to do good, a fondness for destruction at slight risk or a thousand other reasons, began to drift away from it as soon as the going got tough.

The second factor was the surge of prosperity and industrial development in South Africa, accompanied by rising real income for all sectors of the population and by an increasing influx of non-White workers into skilled and semi-skilled occupations that had formerly been reserved for Whites.

Third, and probably most important, was the upsurge of nationalism throughout Southern Africa. Branding South Africa, Rhodesia and the Portuguese possessions as pariah societies, making them wear the leper's bell, abusing them in the United Nations, seeking to crush them by means of boycott and embargo, denying them defensive arms and either tacitly supporting, or affecting blindness toward, the assault on their leaders and their industrial installations by foreign terrorists—these measures did not divide the Whites of Southern Africa, make them hesitate in their course or persuade them to re-examine their motives. On the contrary, they solidified South Africa as the population of a besieged city is solidified when it is ringed by enemies and has its back to the wall. A *Laager* mentality grew with persecution. The Whites were not only united by the threat of external attack, but exhilarated by it. As the external pressures against Southern Africa increased, the non-White population began increasingly to share in the nationalist sentiment. The Communists were no longer regarded tolerantly as reformers of one sort or another, but were deemed to be the relentless, directing core of the coalition of forces seeking to envelop and destroy White Africa.

While conditions in Southern Africa are in some ways unique, an analysis of the rise and destruction of the Communist movement south of the Zambesi may contain useful lessons for other countries. This book deals—I hope factually—with the rise and fall of that movement. It does not concern itself primarily with race relations in Southern Africa or with any of a variety of other problems of interest and importance.

To the extent that race problems are inextricably interconnected with the Communist movement, I have sought to avoid moralizing about Apartheid. It seemed more constructive to examine the historic matrix of existing racial conflicts, to trace the formulation of a South African White ideological consensus and to examine the possible political solutions to the South African ethnic impasse together with their probable consequences and implications. Disapproving, as most Americans do, of the rigid racial separation imposed by the South African White minority, one may still ask one's self whether the United States can be so confident that it has found the solution to the problem of Negro-White relations that it can afford to condemn other nations which have chosen a different path. The rightness or wrongness of the South African Apartheid policy need be only one ingredient in the formulation of United States policy toward Southern Africa. That policy should be based primarily on American national interests and, on these grounds, its fundamental reappraisal seems overdue.

TRAITORS' END

✧ ✧ ✧ ✧ ✧

CHAPTER ONE

Background of Race Conflict

"Even during the worst stresses of the war it was regarded as a nameless crime on either side to set the black man on his fellow foe. . . . I ask the House to remember the gulf which separates the African negro from the immemorial civilization of India and China. The House must remember these things in order to appreciate how the colonists feel toward that ever swelling sea of dark humanity upon which they with all they hate and all they love float somewhat uneasily. . . . This black peril, as it is called in the current discussion of the day, is surely as grim a problem as any mind could be forced to face. Yet it is the one bond of union between the European races who live in the country, the one possibility of making them forget the bitter and senseless feuds that have so long prevailed; and which may have led the people of South Africa to look with a real feeling of self-restraint and comfort to the armed forces of the British Crown."

—WINSTON S. CHURCHILL, *Address to the House of Commons, February 28, 1906*

THE COMMUNIST DRIVE TO DOMINATE AFRICA SOUTH OF THE Zambesi cannot be understood without a few factual comments about this exceedingly complex region, its unique racial *mélange*, its peculiar institutions and its dramatic

and stormy history. This is particularly the case since many
of the confident assertions made about Southern Africa
and its problems rest upon assumptions which are contrary to fact and upon misconceptions born of ignorance
or spawned by propaganda.

The view that the White settlers of South Africa and
their descendants are intruders in a Black man's country
is one of these illusions. When the Dutch landed in Table
Bay more than three centuries ago, Bantu-speaking Negro
tribes had not yet arrived in the area. The Bantu claim to
the land may rest on weight of numbers, but it cannot be
predicated on priority of settlement.

In 1652, some 37 years after the New Netherlands Company built its first storehouse and fort on Manhattan, Jan
van Riebeeck, in command of three vessels, dropped anchor
in Table Bay and established a victualling station for Dutch
ships bound from Europe to the East Indies. Just as the
early settlers of North America expanded territorially
through conflict with the primitive Indian tribes which
possessed the land they coveted, so the Dutch in South
Africa alternated between a symbiotic economic relation-
ship and armed conflict with the indigenous races in possession of southernmost Africa.

Hottentots and Bushmen

These primitive races were not Negroes. They were
Hottentots and Bushmen. Both were primitive pastoral
and hunting peoples, the Bushmen being considerably
more gifted as artists than the Hottentots, but economically more backward. In appearance, these natives of the
Cape and its environs were short to dwarfish, a light yel-
lowish brown in color, with peppercorn hair, eyes protected
by fatty lids from the blazing solar radiation of desert and

karoo country, and skin with an extraordinary tendency to wrinkle. Both groups represented excellent adaptation to desert conditions, their skin being about twice as effective as that of the Bantu in reflecting sunlight. The Bushman women are remarkable for their prominent and everted *labia minora*, which at full maturity may hang down several inches, and for *steatopygia*—enormous, protruding buttocks, the gluteal fat of which is held firmly in place by fibrous tissue. These may serve to store food for foetus and infant during pregnancy and lactation under conditions of uncertain food supply.[1] On the theory that they serve as general food storage bins, these buttocks have been compared with camels' humps and with the fat tails of certain varieties of sheep.

As for the origins and the racial history of the Hottentots and Bushmen, there is a large area of uncertainty. Carleton Coon considers them to be one of the five great races of mankind and asserts that the Capoid race, which they constitute, probably evolved independently from certain *homo erectus* types and, as it trekked southward toward its present habitat, evolved, for reasons that are not entirely clear, in the two directions of dwarfism and *pedomorphism* (or infantile appearance).[2] Other anthropologists regard Bushmen and Hottentots as the products of miscegenation between half a dozen different stocks inhabiting Africa at the time. The evidence from blood groups shows unexpected affinities, particularly very high cDe chromosome frequencies, between Hottentots and Negroes.[3]

[1]Carleton S. Coon, *The Living Races of Man*. New York: Knopf, 1965, p. 112.

[2]Carleton S. Coon, *The Origin of Races*. New York: Knopf, 1962, pp. 636–49.

[3]A. E. Mourant, *The Distribution of the Human Blood Groups*. Oxford: Blackwell, 1954, p. 94.

Unlike the White settlers of North America, the Dutch in South Africa at once proceeded to miscegenate with the Hottentots. Cohabitation was common, marriage rare in the extreme. If the symbol of the Mexican mestizo nation is Malinche, the Indian princess who served as Cortez' interpreter and mistress, a somewhat similar role was played by Eva, a Hottentot convert to Christianity, whose marriage to Pieter van Meerhoff, surgeon and explorer, was the chief social event of the Dutch colony in 1664. Interbreeding with the Hottentots proceeded to such an extent that they eventually disappeared as a racial group. The more warlike and primitive Bushmen were exterminated or driven into the interior where they clashed with the advancing Bantu.

The Coloured or Cape Coloured element in the South African population consists of the two million or so descendants of the mixture of Hottentots with Europeans and with Asiatics who were brought to the Cape to be servants to the Whites. That the rigidly enforced sexual segregation of Europeans and non-Europeans was contrary to the early mores of the colony is illustrated by the fact that Simon van der Stel, one of the most powerful men in the colony at the beginning of the 18th Century, was the son of the Governor of Mauritius by his Asian Indian wife, Monica of the Coast.

The Cape Coloured element in the South African population thus owes its existence to the presence of the White man and is neither of Negro origin nor akin to the Negro socially or intellectually.[4] The Coloured people have no

---

[4]However, a good deal of miscegenation probably occurred between Hottentots and Bushmen and the Xhosa nation of Negroes who today rule the Transkei, since the Xhosa language has clicking sounds that must have derived from Bushman or Hottentot speech.

The Blacks of South Africa belong to a linguistically related group of tribes called Bantu (from the word *Abantu*, meaning people). The older

tribal homelands, nor are they tribally organized. Where the Negroes are primarily herdsmen and subsistence farmers, the Coloured are city dwellers, many of them skilled artisans. The Coloured have no language of their own. Not only do the great majority speak Afrikaans as their native tongue, but they boast of having kept Afrikaans alive when it was threatened with extinction when, under British rule, English became the language of the gentry. Intelligence tests show that the Coloured consistently score higher than the Bantu. However, they are physically weaker. Government policy is to give the Coloured a protected position in Cape Province against Bantu competition and to do everything possible to prevent the destruction of the ethnic identity of this attractive people through intermarriage and miscegenation with the far more numerous Bantu.

At the time of van Riebeeck's landfall at Table Bay, the Bantu were engaged in a centuries-long, frequently interrupted, southward trek, probably from the Ethiopian highlands. They had already entered the Transvaal in the northern portion of the present Republic of South Africa. While the chronology of this migration of small groups of Negroes along a broad front is uncertain, it is probable that the Bantu were south of the Zambesi and hence in Rhodesia by the end of the 14th Century. Succeeding waves enslaved and killed each other. The general rule was that the Bantu killed the Bushmen they encountered, but in what is today South West Africa, the Hottentots subdued the Bantu invaders and reduced them to a miserable and servile existence.[5] It was not until 1770, more

---

generic term *Kaffir* (from the Arabic and meaning "infidel") has been abandoned since it is considered derogatory.
[5]Eric A. Walker, *A History of Southern Africa.* London: Longmans, 3rd edition, 1964, p. 7.

than a century after van Riebeeck's colonization of Cape Town, that the advancing Boer settlers clashed with the Xhosa vanguard of the Bantu beyond the Fish River.

For the next century, an intermittent struggle between the two invading races raged. At Blood River in 1838, Boer Commandos broke the power of the Zulu ruler, Dingane, by slaughtering more than 3,000 Zulu warriors whose bodies were "heaped like pumpkins on a rich soil," while suffering but four wounded and no deaths themselves.[6] Approximately a century after the first encounter, the Zulu nation under Shaka was crushed in the Zulu War of 1879, marking the approximate end of the interracial struggle.

Assimilation, Segregation, Extermination

The race problem in Southern Africa arises in its present acute and perhaps insoluble form because the White settlers failed to deal with the Bantu in a typically Caucasian fashion. In the United States and Canada, the White settlers drove the Indians from their hunting and grazing grounds with superior weapons. While treaties and religious and humanitarian considerations supposedly protected the American Indian, he was inexorably driven from his ancestral lands. The more docile were compressed into reserves, generally comprising poor and inadequate land; the more bellicose were killed. The practice of scalping, which was not an Indian invention since Herodotus reported its prevalence among the Scythians, was an Indian custom that the White settlers enthusiastically adopted as a convenient means of verifying the count of dead Indians for whom bounty was to be paid.

[6]Donald R. Morris, *The Washing of the Spears*. London: Jonathan Cape, 1966, p. 148.

It is all very well to deplore this process on moral grounds, but the alternative would have been to leave one of the richest areas on the face of the earth in the hands of a technically inept people incapable of exploiting it. The failure of the considerable number of Indians who still live miserably on tribal reservations to adjust to modern civilization, despite abundant opportunities and centuries of exposure to it, suggests that, if the Indians had not been ousted from the Great Plains, the latter would have remained under the hoofs of the buffalo.

In Australia, the aboriginal "Black Fellows" were hunted down like rabbits and driven into the desert, where a miserable remnant still survives. The Maori of New Zealand did not fare much better.

The South African experience was different, not because of any moral superiority on the part of the Afrikaners (though this is an illusion that some of them seem to cherish), but for historical and geographical reasons. Both the East Indian Company and the British sought to protect the native populations of South Africa and to ameliorate their conditions of servitude. This caused a violent Boer reaction and a series of treks into the interior to settle new lands and establish self-governing White communities free of the British yoke. The fact that the colony was remote from the world markets, poor in discovered resources and cursed by deficient rainfall, particularly in the hinterland areas of brush and *karoo*, discouraged White settlement. Since the settlers were not numerous, they were unable to rid themselves of British rule and hence impotent to handle the native problem in their own rough way.

While the Bantu might have been driven back into the deep interior, they could not have been made the victims of genocide as were the Maoris and "Black Fellows." They had a continent-wide border across which they could ebb and flow. Moreover, as a race physiologically adapted to work under African tropical and semi-tropical conditions, they represented a potential labor force for the White minority. Nevertheless, Black labor was not effectively exploited in South Africa until the 20th Century. When the coastal lands of Natal were opened up for sugar cultivation, the labor force used was, not the Zulus of the region, but Indians, many of them "untouchables," who were imported under contract from 1860 onward. Similarly, when the Rand gold mines faced an acute labor crisis after the Anglo-Boer War, the preferred solution was not to employ Natives, but to import Chinese.

Thus, the South African solution to the race problem in many ways more nearly resembled that of Spanish and Portuguese America than that of British settlement of the United States and the Dominions. The subordinate Bantu were either relegated to their ancestral reserves or used as a more or less unskilled labor force on farms, plantations and in mines. The salient difference between South Africa and Latin America is that the Afrikaners and other Whites refused to mix their blood with the Bantu and did so only to a decreasing extent with the Cape Coloured and the Indians. As White women became available, either through immigration or natural increase, the taboos on race mixture became more stringent.

The South African solution then had certain points of resemblance to the Indian caste system, which, though extremely complex in its historical development, is based on racial difference, so much so that the Hindi word for caste, varna, means color. But the similarity was by no means complete. The elaborate gradations of caste in

India reflected a society of status in which racial differences were not always either the paramount consideration or evident to the eye.[7] In South Africa, there was only one basic distinction, that between Whites and non-Whites. The concern with color, rather than with race, caste or class, was so intense that the Indian population, though almost certainly primarily Caucasoid, was classified as non-White. In these matters, ethnology has had to yield to political expediency. Thus, the late Prime Minister Hendrik Verwoerd made the extraordinary decision that Japanese were to be considered Whites and Chinese non-Whites. Of course, the two peoples were racially the same. Japan, however, was economically important to South Africa. It was expedient to propitiate her and besides the Japanese colony was small. To have included the Chinese in the White category, however, might have precipitated a similar demand from the Indians. This would have antagonized the European population and particularly that portion of it which was of British descent and imbued with the colonial tradition.

British policy was to protect the Bantu in their established areas of settlement, which assumed the form of a horseshoe, stretching from the northern and eastern borders of South Africa and westward along the coast of the Indian Ocean to Blood River. These areas of dense and preponderant Bantu settlement comprised the best watered and most fertile land. The Whites held fertile areas adjacent to Cape Town, the rich sugar lands of Natal, comparatively bare and semi-arid stretches in the Transvaal and the semi-desert interior or *karoo* that lies in the center of the horseshoe.

[7] Taya Zinkin, *Caste Today*. London: Oxford University Press, 1962.

The Anglo-Boer War and the Poor Whites

The Anglo-Boer War of 1899–1902 constitutes the great divide in South African history. The basic political issue was the desire of two self-governing Afrikaner republics, the Transvaal and the Orange Free State, to remain independent, as against the British will to realize Cecil Rhodes' dream of a great African empire, stretching continuously from Cairo to Cape Town. The economic precipitator of armed conflict was the discovery of fabulous gold deposits on the Witwatersrand, or Reef, in the Johannesburg area of the Transvaal. The mines were owned and exploited primarily by British, and to a lesser extent by Jewish, capital.

The two Boer republics were hostile toward the development of the mines, viewing it as a threat to the democratic and egalitarian society of farmers which they and their ancestors had fought to establish and had trekked by ox wagon into the deep hinterlands to maintain. The farmers of these republics felt their way of life threatened by the development of mining, industry and railroads, by the vices, sophistication and glaring contrasts between opulence and poverty in the new city of Johannesburg. Their attitude was reminiscent of that of Thomas Jefferson, who had dreaded the disappearance of the traditional American society of independent yeomen to make way for the emerging and corrupt world of industry and the metropolis.

Other issues and differences of viewpoint and ideology exacerbated the struggle. The Boers were devout, religious Fundamentalists, imbued with Calvinistic doctrines of predestination and concerned with the God-given duties and obligations of the elect who had been chosen for salvation. They were rural rather than urban, religious rather than scientific, narrowly moral rather than cosmopolitan, the exponents of a frontier democracy rather than of a complexly articulated empire. They believed themselves to constitute a society of equals, consisting of people of the Book—that is to say, the Old Testament—a spiritually elect element with a divine mission to accomplish on earth. They considered themselves the masters and in every respect the superiors of the non-White peoples among whom they lived. Their frequent, long and hazardous journeys into the wilderness in search of what they considered freedom and their numerous and bloody struggles with the Bantu accentuated the parallel which they drew between their historic role and that of the children of Israel between the flight from Egypt and the establishment of Israelite power in Canaan.

The Boer War had some of the ingredients of the two most significant military struggles in American history— the American Revolutionary War and the Civil War. Like the former, it was a struggle of yeomen and farmers to win independence from British rule, in which one of the issues was the desire of the patriots to drive the Natives off arable land and open the entire continent for White settlement. The Boer of 1899, unlike the Confederate of 1861, did not believe in chattel slavery. He did hold that neither equality nor social intimacy between the White and Coloured races was to be tolerated.

In the Civil War, the White South recruited an army of farmers, which represented the almost total mobilization of the adolescent and adult male population of the nation, against a much more professional army, which was more lavishly supplied with matériel and arms, and which was backed by greater industrial power, wealth, population and means of transportation and troop deployment. Against the North's superior physical force, the South relied on such intangibles as morale, courage and *élan*, arising out of the consensus of a homogeneous White democracy that passionately shared a common set of values, ideals and prejudices. The Boer condition was similar. Poorer, more primitive, less populous, sharing a frontier democracy and a commonly accepted way of life, believing in their mission and confiding in divine support, the Afrikaners challenged the most powerful empire on earth and did so with considerable success to the amazement and admiration of Europe and the United States.

At the end of the conflict, there were more British troops on South African soil than the entire male Afrikaner population of the two insurgent states. Viscount Sir Alfred Milner, who served as British Commissioner during the latter part of the war, pursued policies of *Schrecklichkeit* that even surpassed those of General Sherman toward the South. All Afrikaner farms suspected of harboring Boer sympathizers or of having housed Boer soldiers were razed, farmhouses and barns being burned to the ground, fences torn down, livestock driven off and fields left untended. The residents—in almost all cases old men, women and children, since the able-bodied men were fighting—were herded into concentration camps. At the end of the war in 1902, these camps contained some 120,000 White and 80,000 Native inmates. Four thousand Boer women and 16,000 children died in these camps from exposure, disease and hunger.[8] While this terrible mortality was due more to British military callousness and incompetence than to outright sadism, it left scars on the Afrikaner mind that would remain for generations.

[8]Walker, *op. cit.*, p. 498.

At the end of the war, South Africa was impoverished and desolated much as was the South after the collapse of the Confederacy. Agricultural reconstruction was impeded by devastation, pests, bad crop years and surplus population. A large class of Afrikaner poor Whites emerged. Poverty became increasingly conspicuous against the backdrop of gold mine opulence. These poor Whites remained in part a subsistence population in the rural areas, but another large segment migrated to the new, burgeoning cities, particularly Johannesburg, and sought work in the gold mines and in the new industries.

During the next fifty years, the central problem of Afrikaner politics would be to reverse the verdict of the Anglo-Boer War and to transform the poor Whites into a prosperous element, one raised economically, as well as socially and politically, so far above the Native peoples that there could be no danger of substantial admixture.

Considering the recent historical pattern as a whole, the Afrikaner majority has been signally successful in achieving this objective. With few interruptions, political power has been transferred from Britain to South Africa, a process culminating in withdrawal from the British Commonwealth and promulgation of a republic under Verwoerd in 1961. The advance of the Nationalist Party, representing Afrikaner ideology and aspirations, has been continuous since World War II. The virtual Nationalist monopoly of political power has been accomplished by a significant shift of White South Africans of British stock toward support of its program and ideology. Originally a program of emotion and expediency, Apartheid developed under Dr. Verwoerd into a carefully worked out doctrine and program. In its negative aspects, it involves legally imposed racial segregation of a sweeping nature, coupled

with the forcible resettlement of non-White populations
and the elimination of non-White voting rights in the
South African Parliament. In its positive form, it entails
the creation of self-governing Negro tribal councils, or
Bantustans, and the emergence of self-governing councils
and administrative bodies for the Cape Coloured and
Indian peoples.

The South African Alternatives

South Africa's racial problems differ from those of the
United States primarily because of the magnitudes involved. In mid-1967, South Africa had a population of
18.7 million. Of these, 68 per cent were Bantu, 10 per
cent Coloured, 3 per cent Asiatics and only 19 per cent
White. In the United States, by contrast, only about 11
per cent of the population is Negro and yet absorption
of this element into the general population precipitated a
civil war and has caused the White majority enormous
difficulties that continue into the present and show no
signs of abatement.

Given the demographic facts of life in South Africa,
majority rule would inevitably mean Negro rule. It would
not be comparable to domination of American political
life by our own Negro element for two reasons. First, a
very substantial minority of the Bantu are still living
under tribal conditions and a majority of the rest are only
partially detribalized. This involves not merely alienation
from Western Civilization and the problems of a modern
society, but the persistence of such institutions as witch-
craft. Second, the Bantu are about as pure-blooded as
other Negroes of Africa,[9] whereas the American Negroes

[9]George H. T. Kimble, *Tropical Africa.* New York: Twentieth Century
Fund, 1960, Vol. I, p. 86.

are, on the average, somewhere between a fifth and a third White.[10]

With the exception of the Communists and their sympathizers, few South African Whites would accept majority rule under any conditions at any time in the near future. Removal of the White presence, it is believed, would result in a massive economic, social and political retrogression, in a destruction of the high level of civilization that has been attained, in a reversion toward chaos and the jungle and in conditions of lawlessness and genocide comparable to the enormities which have occurred in the Congo and in Nigeria. The Whites also consider that they have an obligation to protect such non-White minorities as the Coloured and the Indians from the probable consequences of majority rule. They recall the events of January 1949 in Durban when a Zulu mob went berserk, murdering Indians and looting Indian shops during two days of rioting in which 147 persons were killed, more than a thousand injured and three hundred buildings destroyed. More recently, East African republics have expropriated the properties of their Indian subjects and then expelled them. Since the Indians are more successful than the Blacks, they constitute what the latter consider to be unfair competition.

An alternate program would be to expel the Bantu from South Africa or else to partition the country into White and Black states and reduce the flow of population between them to a bare minimum. Expulsion of the Bantu is un-

[10]W. S. Pollitzer, *American Journal of Physical Anthropology*, 1958, 16, pp. 241–63; W. S. Pollitzer, R. M. Menegaz–Bock, Ruggero Ceppellini and L. C. Dunn, *American Journal of Physical Anthropology*, 1964, 22, pp. 393–98; D. J. Roberts, *American Journal of Human Genetics*, 1955, 7, pp. 361–67; Bentley Glass and C. C. Li, *American Journal of Human Genetics*, 1953, 5, pp. 1–20; Curt Stern, *U.S. News & World Report*, September 19, 1958, pp. 81–82.

thinkable because they would simply starve. Partition, with subsequent minimal intercourse between Whites and non-Whites, has several possible implications.

First, it is asserted that the withdrawal of Black labor would destroy the gold industry. Actually, if the withdrawal were in stages, it would cause a more rapid trend toward mechanization and automation and might, therefore, benefit the South African economy.

Second, the creation of independent non-White states might involve setting up foci for subversion of White South Africa and could give the White republic a strategically indefensible set of borders as against the relatively clear-cut frontier of the Zambesi, which today separates White from Black Africa.

Finally, South African Whites have a strong sense of duty, stemming from Calvinist indoctrination, toward the non-White peoples of the country. They believe that without White leadership the Bantu would sink into the same sort of insecurity, misrule, poverty, oppression and incipient famine that afflicts much of Black Africa at present. While the Coloured and Indian populations are more capable of self-government, they are socially and economically intermeshed with the White economy. Any complete separation of the races would be a tragedy for the non-Whites.

The most frequently suggested liberal approach to the race problem is that proposed by Cecil Rhodes—"equal rights for all civilized men." Insofar as this means breaking down social barriers to the extent that they apply to educated or successful non-Whites, it is already occurring. The movement in this direction sometimes seems glacially slow, but it is almost certain to acquire increasing momentum.

As a *political* solution, however, Rhodes' proposal runs against the grain of White South Africa. The most fundamental South African objection is to the multiracial state *per se.* A nation is generally defined as a community of people who share a common heritage, institutions, language and loyalty to their native land. These conditions are largely absent in South Africa. The Indians are comparatively recent immigrants partially linked by institutions, religion and history with their Asian homeland. The Bantu regard membership in their tribes and tribe-nations as fundamental and their membership in the South African nation as secondary. Only the Whites and the Coloured meet the requirements of full membership in the South African nation.

Afrikaner political scientists point out that multiracial states generally split into parties or factions organized on ethnic lines. They generally seek maximum advantage for their own groups at the expense of all the others. The centrifugal forces are stronger than the centripetal ones. These nations either dissolve during crisis, as in the case of the old Austro-Hungarian Dual Monarchy or the futile efforts to keep India and Pakistan united after the British withdrawal, or the dominant race, ethnic group or tribal entity resorts to persecution up to and including genocide against the less powerful groups, as in the cases of Rwanda, Sudan, Nigeria and other Black African states.

South Africans occasionally point out that, although Negroes constitute only 11 per cent of the American population, their absorption into the American nation has raised almost insuperable problems. Despite the fact that the entire power of the Federal Government has been exerted to force integration on a sometimes reluctant White majority and despite governmentally enforced preferential treatment for Negroes, the latter are making increasingly strident separatist demands. These range from wearing African dress, being taught a largely mythical and inflated history of their African past and learning Swahili, to establishing communities which are racially segregated against Whites and to striving for Black Power either within the American nation or as a secessionist goal. If the Negro minority constitutes such a massive centrifugal and disruptive force in the United States, where it enjoys full political and legal equality, South Africans ask, what are the realistic prospects of digesting the much more numerous and backward Bantu into the South African state?

The objection to the specific proposal of Cecil Rhodes is that it would not work. The implication is that the franchise should be open to members of all races provided they qualified in terms of education, property, income or some other such criterion. Any system of this sort would be highly unstable as it would run counter to the popular view that the right to vote should be based on biological membership in *Homo sapiens* rather than on responsible citizenship, knowledge or wisdom. Whatever party enjoyed the support of the non-Whites would predictably exert continuous pressure to lower franchise requirements until Black majority rule became an actuality.

In 1966 in Durban, my wife and I explored these possibilities with leaders of the Indian community. These intelligent and attractive people at first advocated Rhodes' solution, but finally reached the conclusion that the end of the process would be Bantu rule and their probable expulsion from the country.

In this complicated and difficult situation, White South Africa has chosen the road of Apartheid, involving the creation of autonomous self-governing states, or *Bantus-tans*, for the major tribal groups of Bantu, such as the Xhosa, Zulus, Bapeda, Sotho and Tswana. The first of these homelands, the Transkei, occupies an area of 16,330 square miles—about the size of Denmark—and contains some of the most fertile and best-watered arable land in South Africa. Regardless of where they live, all South African Xhosas are citizens of the Transkei, entitled to vote in its elections and subject to its laws. Non-Xhosas cannot acquire land or business enterprises in the Transkei or enjoy rights of citizenship there. Existing White businesses and farms are being bought out and sold to Xhosas, often at the cost of economic havoc.

By early 1969, *Bantustans* were in an advanced stage of organization for the Ovambos of South West Africa, the people of the Ciskei and the Tswanas. These homelands are self-governing autonomous areas, but subject to Pretoria in all matters of foreign policy, defense and internal security. In 1966, the Transkei was governed by a Xhosa Cabinet, but the main burden of administration was in the hands of a harassed and overworked corps of White officials. As part of the official drive toward full Bantu self-government, these White civil servants were being rapidly phased out, a process which the elected Xhosa Ministers viewed with understandable alarm.

In 1964, about 42 per cent of South Africa's Bantu population of 11.8 million lived in their tribal homelands, another 34 per cent worked on European farms and the remaining 24 per cent lived in the cities. The goal is to have the Bantu who work on White farms returned to their tribal homelands as farming becomes mechanized and to have Bantu labor in the cities held down to the level of available employment. The main difficulty with this approach is that the urban Bantu had an average income of about $210 per head in 1964 as against approximately $73 on White farms and in the tribal homelands. While income levels have increased considerably since 1964, the ratio has not changed in favor of the rural and tribal Bantu.[11] Thus, Bantu resistance to being extruded from the opulent cities and compressed into the tribal areas is understandable.

The government program involves making the *Bantustans* economically attractive to the Negro population while, at the same time, preventing White economic or political domination of these areas. In the Transkei, considerable progress had been achieved by 1966. However, due to the exceedingly poor agricultural practices of the Xhosas, their unwillingness to abandon traditional ways of doing things and their slowness to learn new techniques, an immensely fertile area, capable of cultivating crops ranging from corn to sugar cane, was not even feeding the 1½ million inhabitants of the area. Japanese agricultural experts who visited the Transkei maintained that the soil could support 3 million people and provide an export surplus if it were tilled by Oriental peasants.

Education is regarded as the main key to progress in the Transkei. Advance in this field was severely limited by an "extreme shortage of well-qualified teachers in the post-primary schools. . . ." The "services of qualified African teachers for the teaching of mathematics, science and Afrikaans were almost unobtainable." It was not even possible "to recruit an African teacher who is qualified to teach commercial subjects even at Junior Certificate

[11]Dr. J. Adendorff, General Manager, Bantu Investment Corporation, "The Economic Development of the Bantu and the Bantu Homelands," address delivered at Durban, February 15, 1965.

level."[12] Despite the fact that the Transkei has been an area of missionary education of the Xhosa since the early 19th Century, only 3.6 per cent of the Negro children attending school were in post-primary grades in 1965. While South African universities graduate Negroes who are competent as lawyers, social workers, ministers, teachers and practitioners of other verbal skills, "very few African students are to be found in technical facilities such as engineering, agriculture, architecture and quantity surveying and only a small number in the faculties of science." In 1960, only 3 per cent of the African matriculants, as against 24 per cent of the Indian candidates, qualified for admission to medical schools.[13]

The experience of the Bantu Investment Corporation, a South African governmental body, has been that only a minority of the most qualified Africans in the Transkei are able to run the local stores and trading posts. Despite the fact that the B.I.C. attempts to train African candidates in bookkeeping and business management, the latter frequently give the stores back to the Corporation on the grounds that they find it impossible to make decisions.[14]

Despite these obstacles to development, there has been undoubted progress in the Transkei and in other tribal homeland areas. Good highways, electricity and technical education are being brought to the villages. The South African Government grants substantial preferential concessions to White industries that will locate or relocate just beyond the frontiers of the tribal homelands. This

[12]Transkei Government, Report of the Department of Education. Umtata: Elata Printers, 1965, pp. 5–7.
[13]S. Biesheuvel, The Human Resources of the Republic of South Africa and their Development. Johannesburg: Witwatersrand University Press, 1963, p. 24.
[14]Interview with Dr. J. Adendorff, General Manager, Bantu Investment Corporation, Pretoria, October 27, 1966.

expedient enables the Bantu to benefit in terms of employment and wages from White capital investment and managerial skill. The White enterprises and their managerial personnel live and work outside the Bantu areas, thus preserving, at least formally, the principle of African predominance in the economic life of the reserved areas.

Realistically speaking, the success or failure of the enormous expenditure of capital investment in the Bantu homelands will not be measured by Western standards, but in comparison with the condition of Black Africa as a whole. Rampant population growth in the Bantu areas may keep living standards close to the present inadequate levels. If, however, during this period, Africa north of the Zambesi and south of the Sahara continues to move toward food crisis and famine, the Bantu homelands may be regarded as successful by comparison.

✧ ✧ ✧ ✧ ✧

CHAPTER TWO

Geopolitics of
Soviet Subversion

"In the groves of *their* academy, at the end of every vista, you see nothing but the gallows."

—EDMUND BURKE, *Reflections on the Revolution in France*

SOUTHERN AFRICA IS A MAJOR TARGET OF SOVIET AND Chinese Communist subversion because of its geopolitical position. A region of vast natural resources, of modern industry and sophisticated technology, it is a bastion of Western Civilization in an ocean of stagnant, backward peoples rooted to a primitive agriculture. Destruction of White rule in Southern Africa would provide the Soviets with a dominant position over the lands between Gibraltar and India, would give them control over the naval base at Simonstown and over the ports of Cape Town and Durban, which control both the Indian Ocean and the Cape route from America to Asia. It would provide gold mining resources sufficient to dislocate the monetary sys-

tems of the West and it would eliminate the one major
strongpoint of free enterprise and representative government in Africa.

This subcontinent of Southern Africa is a unitary, com-
pact region of contiguous territories, stretching from the
Zambesi River to the Cape of Good Hope along its north-
south axis and from the Indian to the Atlantic Ocean in
an east-west direction. It comprises the Republic of South
Africa, the mandated territory of South West Africa, which
South Africa governs, Rhodesia, Portuguese Angola and
Portuguese Mozambique. It has about half the area of the
United States, about one–sixth its population and about
one-fiftieth its White population.

Except for such independent or autonomous areas as
Botswana, Lesotho, Malawi, Swaziland and the Transkei—
all of which are Negro-ruled enclaves or semi-enclaves—
Southern Africa is governed by its White minorities. Of
these countries and territories, the Republic of South
Africa is by all odds the most important and its fortunes
and vicissitudes in confronting Communism will, accordingly, be given much closer attention in this book than
those of its neighbors.

In December 1966, *Fortune* published an article on the
economic development of South Africa entitled "The One
Modern Industrial Complex South of Milan." The geog-
raphy of *Fortune's* editors was deplorable, since New York,
Detroit, Pittsburgh and Chicago all lie south of the Italian
city, but the underlying idea was right. South Africa is the
industrial colossus of the Southern Hemisphere, a burgeoning economic giant, whose economic, social and cultural progress arouses the envy of Black African states,
some of which seem to have moved in one leap from their
birth pangs to their death agonies.

With 4 per cent of the area and 6 per cent of the population of the African continent, South Africa produces about half of its electric power, has half of its telephones and almost half of its cars. Enjoying one of the swiftest growth rates in the modern world, South Africa more than doubled her national income between 1958 and 1967. Total South African national income was estimated officially at $11 billion (U.S. dollars) in 1967.[1] If we assume that approximately 65 per cent of this was distributed to Whites, 5 per cent to Indians and Coloured, and 30 per cent to the Bantu,[2] it follows that White per capita income in 1967 was about $2,010. This is higher than the estimated 1968 per capita income of every European country except Sweden, some 40 per cent higher than British income and more than twice the estimated per capita income of the Soviet Union.[3]

South Africa has the largest and most up-to-date oil-from-coal plant in the world and is able to mine coal and deliver it to Europe at a lower cost than any other producer. She has immense reserves of gold, copper, uranium, coal, chromium and other minerals. She produces two and a half times as much steel per White inhabitant as the United Kingdom. Comparing the entire South African population, two-thirds of which is Bantu and over one-fifth of which is tribal, with the population of the Soviet Union, one finds that South Africa produces 54 per cent more newsprint per capita—an indicator of literacy

[1]*Monthly Bulletin of Statistics*, United Nations, April 1969, p. 187.
[2]South African Institute of Race Relations, A *Survey of Race Relations in South Africa* (compiled by Muriel Horrell), Johannesburg, 1966, pp. 204–05; H. J. J. Reynders and M. van der Berg in *Bantu*, March 1966; *Natal Mercury*, February 16, 1966, citing Ministry of Bantu Administration and Development figures.
[3]Population Reference Bureau, *World Population Data Sheet—1968*, Washington, D.C., March 1968.

and cultural level—and 116 per cent more cars and trucks per head of total population than the U.S.S.R. Even the non-White citizens of South Africa have more cars in proportion to population than the subjects of the Soviet Union.

South Africa has been fortunate in having a built-in stabilizer against deflation and depression in the form of gold production. In times of slump, when prices and hence costs fall, the gold price remains stable, gold profits increase, and mine output, mine employment and bullion exports rise. With the increasing sophistication of international monetary controls, however, gold has become less and less valuable as an economic stabilizer.

The contrast with the economies of Black Africa is revealing. The estimated 1968 per capita income of the Negro states of Africa is $83 yearly as against $259 for the average South African Bantu. The average income of Asians is $128 and of Latin Americans $344.[4] Thus, the South African Bantu earns about three times as high an income as the average citizen of Black Africa and about twice as much as the average Asian. The Rhodesian Bantu earns about twice as much as the citizens of the Black African states. It is estimated that the average Asian Indian in South Africa is four times as well off as the average Indian in India.

The South African "Concentration Camp"

In the United States, one hears the strident voices of the representatives of the putatively liberated states of Black Africa demanding, on the United Nations rostrum and elsewhere, that South Africa, Rhodesia and Portuguese Africa either be suffocated by boycott and embargo or else

[4]Ibid.

shattered by military invasion as punishment for their alleged persecution of non-White populations. South Africa is "a symbol of oppression to the peoples of color throughout the world," according to Dr. Gwendolen M. Carter.[5] Shortly before his assassination, Senator Robert F. Kennedy embarked on an unsuccessful campaign to persuade American firms to close their South African branches in protest against "repressive and discriminatory Apartheid practices."[6] South Africa has repeatedly been denounced as a concentration camp for its Bantu population. A popular Penguin volume by Brian Bunting is actually entitled *The Rise of the South African Reich.*[7] The publishers, with extraordinary lack of candor, neglected to inform their readers that Bunting was a member of the Central Committee of the South African Communist Party before it was banned in 1950, is the son of a founder of that Party and, while living in exile in England, earned his living as an employee of the Soviet news agency Tass.

One of the most obvious characteristics of concentration camps is that they confine their victims and prevent their escape. By this criterion, the Soviet Union might fairly be described as a concentration camp since its laws still punish attempted escape from its borders with death. The Republic of South Africa, by contrast, not only does not hinder its Bantu citizens from emigrating, but welcomes their partial exodus as removing an economic burden. For many years, South Africa offered subsidies to resident Indians on condition that they return to their country of origin.

[5]Gwendolen M. Carter, *The Politics of Inequality.* New York: Praeger, 1962, 2nd printing, p. 11.
[6]Major General Sir Francis de Guingand, *Presidential Address,* Eighth Annual Meeting of the South Africa Foundation, Johannesburg, March 13, 1968, pp. 6–7.
[7]London, Penguin African Library, 1964.

South Africa may be "a symbol of oppression," as Gwendolen M. Carter puts it, to colored intellectuals and politicians, but it is very far from being that to African Negroes. At least, about a million Negroes, who are citizens of other African states, have chosen to live in the Republic. Similarly, in Rhodesia, a large proportion of the detribalized Bantu, who inhabit the towns and work in industry and the mines, are subjects of "free" Black African states such as Zambia and Malawi, where wretched living conditions, massive unemployment, rudimentary public health and education, and insecurity of life and property prevail.

Lenin, in one of his many moments of hard realism, observed that people "vote with their feet." The influx of over a million foreign Africans into the countries under White domination and the continued presence there of tens of thousands of illegal immigrants from the Black states are more revelatory of African realities than the academic propaganda of Professor Carter and other professional opponents of Apartheid.

The primary reason for the population flow is that life offers more hope for the Negro masses in the White-ruled areas. Johannesburg is called *Goldi* by the Bantu for the same reason that European immigrants to the United States half a century ago referred to their destination as "the golden land."

In the field of public education, 1,872,000 Bantu children went to South African schools in 1967, representing 85 per cent of the seven-to-fourteen age group. The literacy rate among the Bantu is 50 per cent as compared with 20 per cent in the rest of sub-Saharan Africa. Approximately 120,000 South African Bantu receive in-service training for Civil Service positions; over 3,300 attended

South African universities in 1967 and more than 3,000 have university degrees.

South Africa spent $9.80 per head of population on public health in 1967 as against an expenditure of 77 cents per capita by Liberia. She boasted a doctor for every 1,800 inhabitants as against one for every 25,000 in Ghana and one for every 40,000 in Liberia. Medical facilities are far superior to those elsewhere on the African continent and Baragwanath Hospital for non-Whites near Johannesburg, with its 85 acres of grounds, 7 miles of corridors, 11 operating theatres and 220 doctors, is the largest in the Southern Hemisphere. Here 6,000 Bantu nurses have been trained and 700,000 out-patients and 100,000 in-patients are treated annually, two-thirds of them gratis.

Whereas most African cities are disfigured by the squalid shacks and hovels in which the masses live, South Africa has virtually eliminated her urban slums. Over the past twenty years, the South African Government has spent $203 million in subsidies for housing for non-Whites. The Soweto development near Johannesburg alone provides 80,000 attractive individual houses with garden plots for Bantu, all equipped with electricity and modern plumbing. Rental for a four-room house is $7.70 per month; water, electricity, sanitation and other services are financed through taxes on employers of Bantu labor; instead of being passive recipients of governmental largesse, the Bantu living in these developments are encouraged to build their own homes on 30-year leaseholds.

The Contrast with Black Africa

Under the much maligned colonial system, Africa was a continent of peace and law, of orderly and steady progress in the midst of a world torn by war and ravaged by totalitarian aggression. Today, much of Africa north of the Zambesi has become a region of endemic corruption, governmental misrule, economic retrogression, insecurity, incipient or actual hunger and genocide. Black Africa was pushed into this maelstrom due primarily to the enthusiasm of British and American liberal politicians for empty generalizations about nationalism and freedom, to their ignorance of the complex realities of the African scene and to their masochistic attitudes and guilt feelings toward non-White peoples. When the dust finally settles, it may well prove to be the case that such well-meaning politicians as Harold Macmillan, Harold Wilson, John F. Kennedy, Robert F. Kennedy and Adlai E. Stevenson will have wrought more havoc and caused more needless suffering in Negro Africa than were occasioned by four centuries of the African slave trade.

The prevalence of genocide in "free" Africa is due primarily to the fact that the basic African units of allegiance are tribal, that the various tribes have been at each other's throats for generations and that the new "nations" of Black Africa represent nothing more substantial than the administrative units of the former European colonies. Thus, when Burundi and Rwanda were given their independence in 1962, the subordinate, but more numerous, Bahutus began a merciless slaughter of the more gifted and aristocratic Watutsi, the tallest people in the world, in which from 8,000 to 25,000 Watutsis were murdered and at least 140,000 became refugees. In Sudan, over a million Negro inhabitants of the southern districts have been massacred or driven out of the country by the dominant Arabs. In Zanzibar, virtually the entire Arab population was murdered, some being buried alive, during and after a Communist uprising. The tribal and political wars that have racked the Congo, in the course of which White settlers have been killed, are too well known to require recapitulation. In Nigeria, the industrious and intelligent Ibos seceded and formed the Biafran Republic to escape genocide. The result was civil war in which the Nigerian Army, after capturing villages, herded Ibo children into huts and nailed the doors shut so they would die of hunger. Up to two million Biafrans have died of starvation.

The new governments of Black Africa have tended to be military dictatorships under omnipotent strong men who are replaced from time to time by means of *coup d'etat* or assassination. The African leaders have found Communist techniques of maintaining dictatorial power and organizing political police systems more useful than the institutions of democracy. For this and other reasons, Communist influence of both the Soviet and Maoist varieties is strong.

Diminution or removal of the White presence has resulted, not only in an enormous increase in insecurity for the African masses, but in economic retrogression. The superb farms of the White highlands of Kenya are disintegrating due to wholesale cattle rustling, encroachment by squatters and reversion to primitive African agricultural practices. There is reason to fear that the famine spots which today exist in Black Africa may expand into a continuous zone stretching from the Zambesi to the Sahara. The prospects for starvation are indicated by the decline in food production while population continues to increase by about 2.3 per cent per annum. According to the Economic Commission for Africa, food output per capita in 1962–63 was estimated to be 4 per cent below the levels prevailing in Africa five years previously. In mid-1966, the Food and Agriculture Organization of the United Nations reported that total African food production per head was 7 per cent below the pre–World War II level. During 1967, according to the U.S. Department of Agriculture, food output rose 3 per cent per head in the Republic of South Africa, but declined by 2 to 3 per cent in the rest of the continent.[8] Four-fifths of the population of Africa consists of agriculturalists, primitive in mentality and techniques, recalcitrant to education and rapidly reverting to the ruinous practices of previous centuries. The 333 million people who inhabit Africa today will increase to 630 million by the end of the century unless wars, pestilence and famine intervene—a prospect that seems highly probable.

Soviet Strategy toward White Africa

Soviet strategy toward White Africa is based not on moral repugnance toward Apartheid, but on realistic considerations of national and ideological self-interest. The fundamental consideration is that the Republic of South Africa is the key to control of the continent. The alternatives are to isolate and weaken it through international pressure or to seize it through military and insurrectionary action. The latter alternative might take the form of a Black People's Republic, to be established by means of invasion or other forms of duress under the aegis of the United Nations. In this strategy, the other component elements of White Africa can be considered as access routes. Rhodesia guards South Africa's northern frontier; South West Africa, Angola and Mozambique are potential invasion corridors from the east and from the west.

[8]G. M. E. Leistner, "Africa and its Future," *Bulletin of the Afrika Instituut,* Pretoria, Vol. V, No. 7 (August 1967), pp. 191–92.

These access countries are more vulnerable to military attack than South Africa itself because they are poorer, industrially much less developed and have smaller White minorities.

The seizure of the advanced South African society intact and the maintenance of its civilization under a puppet Negro republic is obviously an illusory prospect. The White inhabitants of South Africa, Rhodesia and the Portuguese possessions would resist invasion with all the resources at their command. In the unlikely event that the Western powers or the Soviet Union should deploy an invasion force in the area sufficient for military victory, South Africans have indicated that they would pursue a scorched earth policy, leaving little or nothing behind for their conquerors, and then would emigrate.

Without her White population, Southern Africa would probably retrogress into the patterns of tribalism and chaos characteristic of other areas of Negro rule. This prospect, however, is not necessarily obvious to those Negro states that have been launching guerrilla invasion forces against Rhodesia and Portuguese Africa. Similarly, the Arab states harassing Israel may hope to conquer a prosperous country. They refuse to recognize, however, that Israel's wealth is due to the fact that she is inhabited by Jews and not by Arabs.

Thus, if successful, the assault against Rhodesia and South Africa does not involve a mere change in institutions and government, but smashing their highly civilized societies. This may suit the Soviet purpose in Africa. By destroying the one viable center of modern civilization on that continent, the Soviets would be able to expedite the regression of the area into comparatively primitive conditions propitious for Communist rule.

Another reason for the Soviet desire to smash South Africa and Rhodesia is that both countries are committed to the West. South Africa and Rhodesia made major contributions of wealth and blood to two world wars and to the struggle in Korea. In Cape Town, there is a monument to the South African aviators who flew with their American comrades in the Berlin Airlift. The determination of Rhodesia and South Africa to maintain White rule in both countries necessarily implies implacable opposition to both Soviet and Chinese Communism as long as both movements seek to mobilize the non-White masses against European rule.

Another vital consideration is that South Africa produces about three-quarters of the Free World's gold. Control of this, coupled with the not inconsequential gold output of the U.S.S.R., would enable the Soviets to disorganize the international monetary systems of the Western powers. Among other strategic materials at stake is germanium, essential for transistors. The only major sources of supply not behind the Iron Curtain are Katanga and the Tsumeb mine in mandated South West Africa.[9]

From a political standpoint, the crusade against White Africa enabled the Soviets to unite under their political leadership the majority of the Black African states, which viewed South African prosperity with envy and hatred, and the great powers of the West. The latter, particularly during the Administrations of Kennedy and Johnson, reacted with evangelistic zeal to every moral denunciation of South Africa, Rhodesia or Portugal as racist oppressors. As early as 1963, the Communist Party of South Africa continuously reminded its cadres that their own weakness

---

[9]Anthony Harrigan, *Red Star Over Africa*. Cape Town: Nasionale Boekhandel Beperk, 1964, p. 64.

could be counterbalanced by massive international support. The 1963 master plan for Communist conquest of South Africa, *Operation Mayibuye*,[10] stated:

Direct military intervention in South West Africa, an effective economic and military boycott, even armed international action at some more advanced stage of the struggle are real possibilities which will play an important role. In no other territory where guerrilla operations have been undertaken has the international situation been such a vital factor operating against the enemy.[11]

As relations between South Africa and the United States continued to deteriorate during 1961–68, the possibility loomed that the Soviets might maneuver the West into a fratricidal struggle against White Africa, which would further weaken the Free World and provide the Soviet Union and Communist China with the opportunity to launch new adventures of aggression and conquest unhindered.

The role of South Africa in Soviet military and naval strategy became of increasing importance as Soviet influence in the Mediterranean and the Red Sea grew. The Soviet Union has always been aware of the importance of sea power and the control of strategic narrows. Thus, Panamanian Communists organized bloody demonstrations during the Johnson Administration against American control of the Panama Canal. Support of Archbishop Makarios during the Cyprus disturbances of the mid-1960's and the persistent attempts to kindle this conflict into civil war were linked to Soviet naval aspirations in the Mediter-

[10]*Mayibuye* is a Zulu word meaning "return."
[11]Lauritz Strydom, *Rivonia Unmasked!* Johannesburg: Voortrekkerpers, 1965, p. 67.

ranean. Soviet backing of the Egyptian campaigns of terrorism in Yemen and Aden was designed to ensure that
the southern outlet to the Red Sea fell into hands friendly
to the U.S.S.R. after the departure of the British. The
Communist-led bloody upheaval in Zanzibar was presumably related to interest in control of the Madagascar straits.

After the Israeli victory against the Arab states in 1967,
Soviet influence grew to immense proportions in the Near
East. Egypt became a Soviet client state; naval bases became available to the U.S.S.R. in both Egypt and Algeria;
the Soviets openly asserted their naval supremacy in the
Mediterranean and requested American Fleet units to withdraw from the area as intruders. These developments increased the strategic importance of Southern Africa to
both the Western and the Soviet alliances. The naval
implications of this new situation have been stated succinctly and authoritatively by the distinguished military
historian, General S. L. A. Marshall:

When a line is drawn through the top of Africa across the
Arabian peninsula to the corner where Iran meets West Pakistan and with this base, with one point at Karachi and the
other at the Canaries, an isosceles triangle is projected evenly
toward the Cape, much open ocean is enclosed as well as a
twelfth or thereabouts of the earth's surface. With Aden out,
now that the British are yielding it to the Arabs, the only
modern and friendly ports are in South Africa. At Simonstown,
30 miles from Cape Town, is the only great naval base and
graving yard in that quarter of the globe. The United States
must not discount the connection between such a facility and
the conserving of its worldwide strategic interests. In the event
of major war in the Middle East—a struggle over Iraq, for
example—in which our forces became engaged, we would have
to lean on that prop. We have done so before.

The Royal Navy, which takes the practical professional view
of such matters, arranged in 1955 for the naval installations at

Simonstown to be available to its ships when the necessity arises. The radio station at Youngsfield is jointly operated by the Royal Navy and the South African Navy. Annually joint naval exercises are held in the South Atlantic with the ships of Britain, the U.S., other NATO nations and South Africa participating. The only steady watch on Soviet naval excursions into these waters—and there are many submarine sightings—is conducted by South Africa's ships.

Our strategic interest in that corner of the globe continues to expand rapidly. The Navy would like to operate regularly in the Indian Ocean, if it had stretch enough. The uncertainties about Red China, the volatile condition of Indonesia, the Arab takeover in Aden next to the turmoil in Yemen with the increasing likelihood that the Soviets will exploit it and possibly find a base there, along with the heavy involvement of our power in the Indochina war, all militate against making such an extension of our sea power presence desirable. The Navy's main problem today is the management of resources. Since the Tonkin Bay incident, 61 Atlantic Fleet ships and about 70,000 men have been rotated to Vietnam waters for six-to-eight month tours. Some of this movement has been via the Cape, and the South Africans, though called on for friendly assistance, have also been too frequently rebuffed.[12]

The only alternative proposed to the five great ports of Cape Town, East London, Durban, Port Elizabeth and Walvis Bay in South West Africa is Ascension Island in the Indian Ocean. It has no naval base capable of refitting a damaged man-of-war and is far too small to serve NATO fleet requirements in that area.

When the Suez Canal was closed by Egypt after her 1967 defeat at the hands of Israel, South Africa accelerated her ambitious program of harbor improvement to accommodate the increase in traffic. During the next 18 months,

[12]General S. L. A. Marshall, *South Africa: the Strategic View.* New York: American-African Affairs Association, 1967, pp. 4–5.

7,000 to 8,000 ships were diverted to South African ports.[13] In fiscal 1967–68, 42.8 million tons of ocean-borne freight from 55 nations cleared South African ports as compared with the 33.6 million tons handled in 1966–67.[14]

Even if the Suez Canal should be reopened, much of this traffic would never return to the old route. Tankers are being built of over 700,000 tons, as against the 70,000-ton limit for transit through Suez. According to a *Wall Street Journal* analysis, 300,000-ton tankers can deliver oil to Western Europe from the Middle East via the Cape of Good Hope at a cost of $2.33 per ton whereas the smaller tankers going through Suez incur costs of $3.32 per ton.[15] Thus, at a time when U.N. Ambassador Goldberg, who seldom missed an opportunity to harpoon South Africa, was proposing to Secretary of State Rusk that the United States embargo oil shipments to that country, American tankers and American Fleet vessels were using South African ports as part of their lifeline.

[13]*South African Digest*, week ended February 28, 1969, p. 6.
[14]*South African Digest*, week ended March 7, 1969, pp. 1–2.
[15]Cited without date by Marshall, *op. cit.*, p. 10.

❖ ❖ ❖ ❖ ❖

CHAPTER THREE

Birth of the South African Communist Party

"Workers of the World Unite to Keep South Africa White!"
—*Slogan of the striking Rand miners*

DURING THE DECADE FOLLOWING THE ANGLO-BOER WAR, the swift rise of the gold mining industry on the Rand created an industrial working class and a radical labor movement. The mines attracted skilled trade unionists from Great Britain and Afrikaner poor Whites whose farms had been ravaged by three years of war, followed by drought. These White workers were exposed to the various radical doctrines prevalent in Europe and the United States: British trade unionism and Fabian socialism, the industrial union philosophy of the Knights of Labor and the I.W.W. (Industrial Workers of the World), Marxism, De Leonism and the militant popular nationalism of the Boer Commandos.

The labor movement championed the preeminent position of White workers as against non-Whites. It was accepted as a matter of course that each White miner should have a Black man to carry his tools and do the heavy, unskilled work. Where the White man earned a pound a shift, the Black man received two shillings—or a tenth as much.[1]

There was a basic cleavage between the mine owners and the White labor organizations concerning the role of non-White workers. As early as 1879, Sir Bartle Frere, a staunch advocate of British empire in Africa, had foreseen the dangers of creating a poor White working class and had predicted that "the more educated and misguided Boers, dominated and led by better educated foreign adventurers—Germans, Hollanders, Irish Home Rulers, and other European Republicans and Socialists—would become a pest to the whole of South Africa." As for Cecil Rhodes, he had stated bluntly: "We do not want a White proletariat in this country. The position of the Whites among the vastly more numerous Black population requires that even their lowest ranks should be able to maintain a standard of living far above the poorest sections of the population of a purely White country."

With the Boer War over and the Rand safely in British hands, the mine owners became concerned with the need for cheap labor in continuously increasing quantities. Skeptical of their ability to recruit Bantu in the requisite numbers and dubious of the aptitude of these tribal Africans for mine work, they proceeded to import Chinese coolies, and by 1906 some 50,000 were working in the Witwatersrand. Since there were large numbers of unemployed Whites in the Rand, the South African Labor Party, led

[1]R. K. Cope, *Comrade Bill: The Life and Times of W. H. Andrews, Workers' Leader*. Cape Town: Stewart Printing Company, undated, pp. 27–28. This is an official biography of one of the main founders and leaders of the South African Communist Party.

by F. H. P. Creswell, agitated to deport the Chinese and use White workers for all skilled and semi-skilled jobs. Creswell ran for the Transvaal Parliament on this issue in 1907, but was narrowly defeated.

In Britain, emotional agitation against "Chinese slavery" swept the country and the Earl of Balfour, the Unionist leader and former Prime Minister, even urged that the evil be stamped out by armed force. The young Winston Churchill, who was serving as Under-Secretary at the Colonial Office, was unimpressed by this intense moral indignation. "A labour contract into which men enter voluntarily for a limited and for a brief period," he told the House of Commons, "under which they are paid wages which they consider adequate, under which they are not bought or sold and from which they can obtain relief on payment of seventeen pounds ten shillings, the cost of their passage, may not be a healthy or proper contract, but it cannot in the opinion of His Majesty's Government be classified as slavery in the extreme acceptance of the word without some risk of terminological inexactitude."[2]

When the Liberals won an election on the issue of ending Chinese "slavery," they found only a handful of the "slaves" had any desire to return to China. Thus, they were compelled to rescue the Chinese by forcefully deporting them.

During the years prior to World War I, South Africa developed a strong trade union movement, one more prone to violence than its British counterpart, and a Labour Party, founded in 1909. The salient difference between this labor movement and those of Europe and the United States was its ardent championship of Apartheid, White

[2]Randolph S. Churchill, *Winston S. Churchill*, Vol. II, *Young Statesman: 1901–1914*. Boston: Houghton Mifflin Company, 1967, pp. 162–63.

supremacy, the color bar and the reservation of all skilled and semi-skilled jobs for Caucasians.

Founders of South African Communism

The most influential founder of the South African Communist Party, William Henry Andrews, emerged from this trade union and labor movement. Born in Suffolk in 1870 into the "aristocracy of labor," he proceeded to South Africa because of the depression of 1892 in England and the tales of fabulous wages to be earned by skilled White workers on the Reef. The trip in those days was by Union Castle liners, which, aided by large square sails, made the passage from London to the Cape in seventeen days—only three days more than the voyage takes today by freighter.

Andrews began trade union organization in 1894 and was elected president of the Trades and Union Council in 1903. At the time, Afrikaner poor Whites were living in shanties on the outskirts of the main cities of the Transvaal and Orange Free State. Hungry Boer women with their infants in their arms demonstrated for relief before the Bloemfontein Assembly in 1908, but were turned aside. Health conditions in the mines were wretched and the danger of tuberculosis was so great that labor leaders estimated that a drill operator could count on an average working life of only five years.[3]

These miserable conditions created an explosive situation from which both trade union leaders and Afrikaner Nationalists profited. In 1907, Andrews led a mass strike of White gold miners in the Rand in which the workers resorted to wholesale sabotage, blew up mine property with dynamite and left holes in their boilers so the "scabs"

[3]Cope, *op. cit.*, p. 90.

who took their jobs would be killed.[4] The strike was broken with military force, but Andrews had induced British and Boer workers, despite their bitter memories of war and for the first time in South African history, to cooperate in common action.

Meanwhile, an intellectually more distinguished future founder of the South African Communist Party had struck roots in his adopted country. Born in London in 1873, Sidney Percival Bunting graduated from Oxford, winning the Chancellor's Prize for Classics, and came to South Africa in 1900, probably as a British soldier in the Anglo-Boer War. He descended from a distinguished family, which combined Puritanism, an exalted sense of duty and a propensity to devote themselves to movements in favor of the downtrodden. His great-grandfather, Jabez Bunting, had been the acknowledged leader of Methodism in Britain. His father, Percival William Bunting, founded the *Contemporary Review*, was knighted and, with his wife, toured England and the Continent in behalf of women's rights.[5]

Settling in South Africa after the war, Bunting became an unsuccessful lawyer. He at first sided with the mine owners, but later was won over by Creswell to the latter's program of creating a White labor movement, from which the non-White workers would be excluded. In 1909, he became an officer of the White Expansion Society, dedicated to stimulating European immigration and settlement.

In the summer of 1914, on the verge of World War I, a strike again raged in the Rand mines. Some 19,000

[4]*Ibid.*, p. 92.
[5]Edward Roux, *S. P. Bunting, A Political Biography*. Cape Town: The African Bookman, 1943, pp. 9–13.

workers joined the movement, of which William Andrews
was a principal leader. White miners went into the com-
pounds and told the Bantu workers to down tools or be
dynamited. The attitude toward non-strikers was expressed
succinctly by George Mason, leader of the carpenters:
"There is no scab for which there is not a pond large
enough to drown him or a rope long enough to hang his
carcass." Lists of scabs were posted throughout the Rand
to be tried, condemned and put to death by strikers' vigi-
lante groups. After a bloody clash between strikers and
police in Johannesburg, a general strike was called and a
pro-labor mob set fire to the railway station and to the
offices of the *Star*, a newspaper unfriendly to the strikers'
methods and cause.

Gradually, the strike began to assume the aspects of an
armed uprising. Red flags were displayed and gunshops
were looted for arms. The authorities decided against putting down the movement with military force on the
theory that the cost in lives would be excessive and the
protection of innocent people outside the cities difficult,
if not impossible. At the cost of 21 civilians and six police
and military killed, the miners won a partial victory.

The somewhat inarticulate Bunting, whose sentence
structure was complex and delivery halting and inept, took
no active part in this movement, but observed from the
sidelines what he hoped would be "the first act of South
Africa's working-class revolution, whose end is not yet."[6]

From World War to Comintern

As in Europe and America, World War I split the
South African Socialist and labor movement. In 1913, the

[6]Roux, *op. cit.*, p. 19.

South African Labour Party had affiliated with the Second International and endorsed the latter's Stuttgart anti-war resolution. On August 2, 1914, when war had already started on the Continent but two days before Great Britain's declaration of hostilities, the Administrative Council of the Labour Party, under the chairmanship of Andrews, blamed "the capitalistic governments of Europe" for fomenting a conflict "which can only benefit international armament manufacturers' rings and other enemies of the working class." South African labor was urged to "refrain from participating in this unjust war."[7]

Frederic Creswell, the leader of the Labour Party, promptly announced his support of the war and was backed by the Party publication, *The Worker*. After some hesitation, Andrews went into opposition. He was one of the two chief leaders of the Party and had no desire to split it. Moreover, he knew that most labor leaders leaned toward support of the Government and that the anti-war element consisted mainly of middle-class intellectuals and shopkeepers, and was more motivated by humanitarian considerations and Marxist doctrines than by any concern with the welfare of the workers. Having no real rapport with organized labor, Bunting hurled himself into the anti-war movement and, together with P. R. Roux, father of his future biographer, organized the War on War League in 1914.

In late August 1914, Creswell called a special conference of the Labour Party in Johannesburg at which a majority of 82 to 30 agreed to "support the Imperial Government wholeheartedly in the prosecution of the War." The Administrative Council of the Labour Party demanded a

---

[7]Cope, *op, cit.*, p. 162.

pledge of loyalty to the Government on pain of expulsion. Andrews refused and was forced out of the Party.

The dissident group formed the International Socialist League (ISL), into which the War on War League dissolved. With Andrews as its chairman, the ISL developed into the nucleus from which the Communist Party of South Africa would sprout. The organ of the new revolutionary movement, *The International*, was placed under the editorship of David Ivor Jones, a consumptive intellectual of ability who was to found the South African Communist Party and die of his disease a few years later in Soviet Russia. In its first issue, *The International* announced that it would dedicate itself to working for international socialism and anti-war unity and for the preservation of Socialist principles.

At the instigation of Bunting and Jones, the ISL moved decisively toward a negrophile position. On October 1, 1915, Jones wrote in *The International*: "An Internationalism which does not concede the fullest rights which the Native working class is capable of claiming will be a sham. One of the justifications for our withdrawal from the Labour Party is that it gives us untrammelled freedom to deal, regardless of political fortunes, with the great and fascinating problem of the Native."

The unpopularity of these views was demonstrated in the "khaki elections" of 1915 in which Andrews, running for Parliament as a candidate of the International Socialist League, received only 140 votes. Roux attributed this miserable showing "not merely to the general unpopularity of the anti-war cause but also to the League's openly pro-Native policy."[8]

Despite opposition even within its own leftist ranks

[8]Roux, *op. cit.*, p. 31.

from Socialists who averred that there was no such thing
as a Native problem, but merely a general workers' problem, the ISL took the unprecedented step of admitting
Black men to its membership and meetings and even
having them address its gatherings. In July 1917, the
Socialists began organizing Bantu cadres to "study the
working-class movement" and soon the idea of an all-
embracing non-White union, modelled on the American
I.W.W., began to assume shape.

In June 1918, the ISL launched a so-called bucket strike
by the Johannesburg Negroes who carried off the sewerage.
When these Bantu workers downed buckets, demanding
a wage increase of sixpence or a shilling a day (accounts
differ as to the exact amount), all 152 strikers were arrested
and sentenced to two months imprisonment under the
Master and Servants Act. "While in jail," the chief magistrate of the court declared, "they would have to do the
same work as they had been doing, and would carry out
that employment with an armed escort, including a guard
of Zulus armed with *assegais* and White men with guns.
If they attempted to escape and if it were necessary, they
would be shot down. If they refused to obey orders, they
would receive lashes as often as might be necessary to
make them understand that they had to do what they
were told."[9]

In a long statement on the race question, Andrews committed the ISL to treat the Native as "part of the working
class," to include him "in the industrial organizations of
the industry in which he is for the time engaged" either
through parallel or integrated unions, the ideal being the
latter, to give him civil equality by abolishing "all special
laws based on race," and to consider intermarriage between

[9]*Cape Argus,* Cape Town, June 11, 1918.

Whites and Blacks "entirely an individual matter. . . ."[10]

These views were regarded as unspeakably abhorrent by the great majority of South African workers. In the June 1917 elections for the Transvaal Provincial Council, Andrews did not dare to run in the British working-class district that had formerly elected him and ran instead in the heavily Jewish Commissioner Street district of Johannesburg. Even though leaflets were printed in Yiddish as well as English, the ISL candidate got only 71 votes.

The ISL was invited to send delegates to the Stockholm conference against war, a revolutionary international gathering energetically supported by Lenin and the Bolsheviks. Its purpose was to turn the "imperialist war" into proletarian revolution. A tumultous meeting in Johannesburg, at which the various factions hurled insults at each other, chose Andrews as the ISL delegate to Stockholm. The Allies, however, used their control over ship movements to the Swedish capital to prevent the delegates from getting there. The meeting was never held and Andrews got only as far as London. In Britain, he met Gallagher, a future leader of the British Communist Party, the radicals who were running the Independent Labour Party, Oliver Schreiner, a gifted South African novelist who had by now become a zealous Communist, and last, but not least, Maxim Litvinov, the Soviet representative in London. The latter indoctrinated him thoroughly, as a result of which Andrews was able to write a pamphlet entitled *The Workers' Revolution in Russia,* which was printed in English, Afrikaans and Yiddish and distributed by the thousands in South Africa. Returning to his country, Andrews was characterized by the press as the "Bolshevik leader of South Africa." He announced on his arrival at

10Cope, *op. cit.,* pp. 182–83.

Cape Town: "I am not a pacifist. I never signed the war-on-war pledge. If I was in Russia, I would be in the Red Guards."[11]

The ISL enthusiastically hailed the Bolshevik Revolution and, because of the impact of that remarkable event on a war-weary country, membership began to revive. Yet by January 1919, more than a year after Lenin's seizure of power in Petrograd, it boasted only a few hundred members.[12] Communist propaganda was printed and disseminated in Zulu, but, after the stern repression of the bucket strike, the Negro trade unions had begun to fall apart. At a time when the world seemed to them ready to be engulfed by Bolshevik revolutions, the South African comrades had more exciting things to do than to try to organize a backward race, work at best so frustrating that those who dedicated themselves to it sometimes felt, as Simón Bolívar put it, that they were "ploughing the seas."

In 1919, a strike of Johannesburg municipal workers broke out in which the striking streetcar operators decided to gain public sympathy by keeping the trams running. The committee entrusted with this activity they dubbed a "soviet." This aroused Bunting to write a tendentious article in which he demonstrated why the committee could not properly be called a soviet in the Leninist sense of the word. He also scolded White labor for having failed to help the luckless Bantu bucket workers a year before.

"The Johannesburg lunch-time crowd," Bunting wrote, "many of them no doubt Trade Unionists fresh from cheering Bolshevism in the Town Hall, not only jeered at the outrages, but helped to catch and belabor any male or female Native luckless enough to be abroad at the time,

[11]Cope, *op. cit.*, p. 193.
[12]Roux, *op. cit.*, p. 39.

proceeding afterward to mob the editor of this paper as a presumed sympathizer with their victims. . . ."

He inveighed against South Africans for "taking up this White-against-Black red herring." Since Bunting was unencumbered by a sense of the ridiculous, he could mix metaphors without restraint. Expounding his favorite theme, that White and Black workers were kept apart due to the machinations of capitalism, he concluded with the warning: "Well, well, then, go on in your old ruts: let your Native fellow workers, like the Russian *moujiks*, be more progressive than you, and, if you will not help their advance, let them advance without you and in spite of you."[13]

This was a good, orthodox Marxist-Leninist analysis of the problem and it is probable that Bunting believed fervently in its truth. But was it actually in the interests of the White workers to draw the Blacks into a common trade union movement? Would the Whites really benefit economically by having the Native workers trained to their level of skill and put in competition with them on the principle of equal pay for equal work? Did the White worker gain nothing from color-bar legislation, which helped keep his wage at ten times the Bantu level and which ensured that no non-White person should ever be put in a position where he could give orders to a White man? Were the capitalists really behind the White supremacy color-bar legislation or did they dread the emergence of a White working class, which could become a source of perpetual class and racial strife?

These and similar considerations should have occurred to a man of Bunting's education and intelligence. If they eluded him, it was because dogmatic zeal and enthusiasm

13Roux, *op. cit.*, p. 44.

for a secular cause had blinded him just as zeal and enthusiasm for a religious cause had blinded some of his ancestors. Bunting, with all his gifts, lacked an analytic mind. He had done poorly in philosophy at Oxford, had found the emotionalism of Marx's *Communist Manifesto* more to his liking than the abstruse paragraphs of that author's *Das Kapital* and had considered Robert Browning his favorite poet.

The ISL coasted along for two years on the prestige of the Bolshevik Revolution. It obtained its warmest reception among the South African Jews, concentrated in Johannesburg. These were largely of Lithuanian origin, had come to South Africa as refugees during the era of intense Czarist persecution, which stretched from 1881 to 1917, and had become very successful as large and small businessmen. In 1916, Bunting married a Jewish refugee of Baltic origin, Rebecca Notlowitz, who worked with him first in the ISL and later in the South African Communist Party.

The Jewish community preserved its interest in Russian developments, its hatred of the autocratic Czarist regime and its warm sympathy for the Russian revolutionary movement. When the Russian Revolution failed to spread over the earth in accordance with the fervent predictions of Lenin and Trotsky, however, Jewish interest in the ISL began to wane.

By January 1919, the International Socialist League consisted merely of branches on the Rand, in Durban and Pretoria, an affiliated group in Cape Town and an ultra-revolutionary, anarcho-syndicalist organization that called itself the Industrial Socialist League.

The First Congress of the Communist International, which met in Moscow in March 1919, considered that the

ISL was so close to its principles that it was eligible for membership without any constitutional or organizational changes, and in 1920 the ISL was admitted to the Comintern.[14]

Hopes for World Upheaval

Neither the Soviet Union nor the Comintern was particularly interested in South African developments during the stormy years between 1917 and 1923. During this period, Lenin believed that Communism was about to sweep first through Europe and then through the rest of the world. The colonial and peripheral countries were obviously destined to play secondary roles in these momentous events and the eyes of the Bolshevik leadership were concentrated on Germany, France and Italy and on the Balko-Danubian states, which constituted a barrier between Soviet Russia and a defeated Germany hopefully on the verge of revolution.

Soviet republics were formed in Bavaria and Hungary in 1919 and, even though both were to prove ephemeral, world revolution seemed at hand. In the first issue of *The Communist International*, its editor, Gregory Zinoviev, wrote: "As we write these lines, the Third International already has as its main foundation three soviet republics— in Russia, in Hungary and in Bavaria; but nobody will be surprised if, when these lines come to be printed, we have not three but six or even more soviet republics. Old Europe is rushing toward revolution at breakneck speed. In a twelvemonth, we shall already have begun to forget that there ever was a struggle for Communism in Europe,

[14]*Der I. Kongress der Kommunistischen Internationale.* Hamburg, 1920, pp. 17–18.

for in a year the whole of Europe will be Communist."[15]

This euphoric mood continued throughout the Second World Congress, which met in the summer of 1920 in Moscow at a time when the victorious forces of the Red Army under Marshal Tukhachevsky were advancing on Warsaw. It seemed to the Communist leaders that the anti-Soviet Polish state under Marshal Pilsudski was about to be overwhelmed, thus uniting Soviet Russia with the German proletariat, "the most advanced" in Europe.[16]

Under these circumstances or, more correctly, under this misapprehension of the circumstances, Lenin insisted that all parties that wished to join the new international accept 21 conditions that he had drafted. These provided that they all assume the title "Communist Party," that they split with all wavering and reformist groups and denounce all reformist leaders as enemies of the revolution and, finally, that they build effective underground organizations equipped for the illegal struggle for power. Each Communist Party was informed that it had a fundamental duty to create "at all costs parallel organizational machinery which, at the decisive moment, will come to the help of the Party in fulfilling its duty toward the revolution."

Lenin demanded this complete rupture with reformists and social democrats in the conviction that they would inevitably, at the critical juncture, betray the revolutionary movement either by vacillation or by outright acts of disloyalty. On the eve of revolution, it was vitally necessary, he believed, that the Communist Parties purge their ranks of elements that would draw back from the armed struggle for power. Lenin's demand that the parties create

[15]*Die Kommunistische International*, No. 1, pp. 9, 12. Quoted by Guenther Nollau, *International Communism and World Revolution*. New York: Praeger, 1961, p. 46.
[16]Nollau, *op. cit.*, p. 49.

illegal organizations parallel to the legal ones was simply a directive that the worldwide Communist movement prepare forthwith for civil war.

The impact on South Africa of the 21 conditions and of the directives to prepare for the struggle for Soviet power vas to torpedo all efforts to reunite the Labour Party now tl at the issue that had caused the schism, World War I, vas no longer relevant. As a Leninist organization, the ISL refused to have any dealings with Creswell and the other Labour Party leaders who had supported their country's war effort. Andrews, probably the most dogmatic and obedient of the founders of South African Communism, wrote in *The International*: "The S.A.L.P.[17] must be attacked, exposed and driven where it belongs, into the arms of reaction and the upholders of the capitalist regime. The I.S.L. will continue its work of agitation and organization of the masses, irrespective of race, colour or creed, on class lines, to fight and destroy the system responsible for the present world misery—peacefully if possible, by force if needs be."

On January 2, 1921, a hundred delegates from the various South African revolutionary organizations met in Johannesburg to launch a "strongly disciplined and centralized" Communist Party. The Social Democratic Federation, the Jewish Socialist Society, the Durban Marxist Club and the Cape Communist Party agreed to join in this new organization, which was to meet Lenin's 21 conditions. On July 29, 1921, the Inaugural Congress of the Communist Party of South Africa (CPSA) met in Cape Town City Hall before an enthusiastic crowd of about 2,000. Andrews was named Secretary and C. B. Tyler Chairman of the Party. The other members of the leading

[17]South African Labour Party.

committee were Bunting and his wife, T. Chapman, J. den Bakker, R. Gelblum, A. Goldman, H. Lee, E. M. Pincus and R. Rabb, together with three representatives from the Cape, Natal and Orange Free State branches of the orgɑnization, whose names were not publicly disclosed.

Thus in a primarily Afrikaner society, only one Communist leader bore a Dutch name. The movement had no figures, with the exception of Andrews and Tyler, who had stature or wielded power in the trade union movement. Moreover, of those who enthusiastically participated in its gatherings, a substantial proportion was police officers in plain clothes.[18]

[18]Cope, *op. cit.*, p. 209.

✦ ✦ ✦ ✦ ✦

CHAPTER FOUR

The Rand Rebellion

"All the armed prophets have been victorious, while the unarmed
prophets have come to grief. . . . No doubt the armed prophets
encounter great difficulties, and they are assailed en route by all
the dangers of their undertaking . . . but, when once they have
overcome them, and have begun to evoke veneration, thanks to
having wiped out all their inveterate detractors, they then remain
puissant, secure, honored and happy ever after."

—Niccolo Machiavelli, *The Prince*

From the beginning, Jan Christian Smuts and the
Unionist Party, which reflected the views of the pro-British minority in South Africa, regarded the rising Communist movement as a hostile and subversive force. As
early as 1919, Red meetings were broken up at Cape Town
and Communist speakers were arrested. Prison terms were
given Reds convicted of printing and distributing literature
in Zulu designed to arouse the Negroes to rebellion. When
two Russians, Lapitzky and Sosnovik, harangued a radical
meeting in Johannesburg and demanded support of the
Bolsheviks in the civil war then raging in Russia, they were
deported.

The leaders of the Nationalist Party took a very different attitude. They viewed Bolshevism at first with pronounced sympathy, regarding it as a nationalist, anti-capitalist movement similar to the struggle they had waged and lost against British imperial rule. Thus, the Boer general, J. B. M. Hertzog, the outstanding Nationalist leader of the time and a future Prime Minister, informed a Pretoria meeting in 1919 that Bolshevism was "the will of the people to be free" and added that some people wanted "to oppress and kill Bolshevism" because "national freedom means death to capitalism and imperialism." Dr. Daniel François Malan, another Nationalist leader and future Prime Minister, declared that the Bolshevik goal was "that Russians should manage their own affairs without interference from outside . . . the same policy that Nationalists would follow in South Africa."[1]

Social unrest swept South Africa in the wake of postwar economic crisis. The ISL and later the Communist Party did everything within their power to capitalize on these movements and propel masses of striking and demonstrating workers, both Black and White, from one stage of revolutionary action to the next in the hopes of gradually developing the force, fervor and ideological conviction necessary for armed insurrection. In 1919, Native strikes, riots and pass-burnings, directed by the African National Congress, but assisted by the Communist Party, swept the nation. In February 1920, the gold mines faced the largest strike of Bantu workers in South African history. With 70,000 Native workers out, Prime Minister Smuts mused

[1]Brian Bunting, *The Rise of the South African Reich.* London: Penguin African Library, 1964, pp. 34–35. Written by the son of Sidney Percival Bunting, this book is generally tendentious in its conclusions, but accurate as to detailed facts.

about the fact that these Blacks were "well organized, picketing and doing things that we would have considered Natives incapable of doing."

The Communists exhorted the White workers to support the strike. In an eloquent *Don't Scab* leaflet, Bunting claimed that the Bantu workers "cannot rise without raising the whole standard of existence for all. He saw the Native strike as harbinger of a great social transformation and claimed that the Bantu were "entering the world-wide army of labour" and "putting aside sticks and *assegais*" in order to learn how to "win the respect of White people by peaceful picketing and organization."

Neither the White union leaders nor the rank and file had any inclination to support the Black strikers. On the contrary, White trade unionists were recruited on a large scale as special constables to maintain order and force the Bantu back into the mines. In his leaflet, Bunting inveighed against this practice: "DON'T SCAB! DON'T SHOOT! Don't take a rifle against your own hammer boys,[2] and see that if the Natives are sent back to their *kraals*, they go by train, where they may be under public inspection all the time."[3]

Bunting and the Communist Party argued that the Chamber of Mines was plotting to "use the crisis to break the White unions" by first starving the Native workers into submission and then doing the same to the White trade unionists. In reality, the mine owners generally favored raising skills, opportunities and wages of the Bantu workers, thus replacing the less skilled element among the Whites who constituted high-cost and somewhat intrac-

[2]The hammer boys were the Bantu unskilled laborers who carried the White miners' tools down into the pits.
[3]The implication was that the Bantu were in danger or being beaten up or killed by the White constabulary.

table labor. The opposition to either improvement or regularization of the status of the Black workers as a permanent labor force in the industry came from White labor. As Bunting's biographer sorrowfully conceded, the *Don't Scab* pamphlet fell on deaf ears.[4]

Beginnings of the Rising

By 1921, the mines were in a difficult situation. Miners' wages were high and the trade unions strong enough to prevent cost economies and modernization. At the same time, high-grade ore was being depleted.[5] In December, the mine owners announced that the status quo agreement, which prevented the hiring of non-White to replace White workers in 19 protected occupations, would have to be suspended because of adverse economic conditions. Four thousand White workers were affected and the others felt their jobs jeopardized by the owners' assertion of full freedom to employ non-Europeans in semi-skilled positions. On January 1, 1922, the mines cut the wages of White workers 5 shillings per shift.

These actions fell with cruel force on the Afrikaner poor Whites, people who were already living in dire misery and squalor. As country folk who had farmed dust-bowl acres, they lacked the education and training for skilled jobs. While they did for the most part rough labor in the mines, they earned White men's wages. There was always the prospect that the less capable among them might be replaced by Cape Coloured or Bantu labor.

The Chamber of Mines forecast that, unless drastic economies occurred, almost two-thirds of the producing

[4]Roux, *op. cit.*, p. 48.
[5]J. C. Smuts, *Jan Christian Smuts*. New York: Morrow, 1952, p. 227.

mines might have to go out of production, throwing 10,000 Europeans out of work in an age when unemployment insurance was non-existent. The Chamber gave formal notice to terminate the status quo agreement.

The response of the workers was a strike of gold miners, coal miners and engineers. By late January, some 20,000 Europeans were out on strike and about 180,000 Natives involuntarily idled.[6] The strike was a combined operation of the skilled British workers, with their trade union traditions and Socialist or Communist sympathies, and the Afrikaner semi-skilled, with their bitter memories of the Anglo-Boer War and their Commando training.

The fledgling Communist Party and its members "flung themselves wholeheartedly into the struggle," but Bunting had "reservations" and moral scruples.[7] He was deeply concerned about the fact that the primary goal of White labor was to preserve and reinforce the color bar. He wandered gruffly among the crowds of strikers, criticizing the movement and selling copies of *The International*. He was never asked to address strike meetings.

Andrews, by contrast, was in the forefront of the struggle. He organized a Council of Action to propel the industrial conflict into a general strike, one that might serve as the overture to an armed struggle. The Action Council members were leftists who had been expelled from the Miners' Union for conducting a previous illegal strike. While not all of them were Communists, the Council was under Communist Party control.[8]

After the Rand revolt was put down, the Martial Law Inquiry Judicial Commission of the South African Gov-

6Walker, *op. cit.*, p. 589.
7Roux, *op. cit.*, pp. 51–52.
8Cope, *op. cit.*, p. 244; Walker, *op. cit.*, p. 591.

ernment found that power had fallen from the "nerveless hands" of the official strike committee, the so-called Augmented Executive, to be seized by men who "though their ultimate aims may have differed, were united for the moment in their determination at all costs to overthrow the Government of the country." The Commission identified these revolutionaries as the leaders of the Council of Action and the Communist Party in Johannesburg.

The International declared officially that, without "necessarily identifying itself with every slogan heard in this strike, the Communist Party of South Africa gladly offers its assistance to the Strike Committee, convinced that essentially this is a fight against the rule of the capitalist class. . . ."

If the Council of Action was a Communist-controlled organ of power, its rival was the Commandos, a paramilitary organization of Afrikaners. Tracing their origin back to the Anglo-Boer War, these Commandos were volunteer detachments under elected military leaders who combined strike action with guerrilla warfare. First formed on the third day of the strike, the Commandos spread the length and breadth of the Rand, or the Reef, as the British called it. With dispatch riders, patrols and arms often stolen from police posts, under the leadership of veteran Boer combat veterans, they were a powerful instrument used to terrorize Negroes, kill "scabs" and engage in pitched battles with the authorities. Wherever they took over, Smuts' son reported, "their trail [was] marked by violence and even murder. Mine officials and some Natives were clubbed or shot in cold blood. There were acts of pagan brutality."[9] The Communist Party eagerly supported the Commandos and offered to instil them with discipline, a

[9] J. C. Smuts, *op. cit.*, p. 229.

strange proposal for civilians without military experience
to make to veterans of a three-year war.

Under Tielman Roos, leader of the Nationalist Party
in the Transvaal, the Commandos, representing, in their
overwhelming majority, the disinherited poor Afrikaners,
organized an impressive mass meeting to demand an end
to British rule and the creation of a South African republic. The Afrikaner farmers enthusiastically supported both
the strike and the Commandos. They regarded the former
as a blow against the hated mine owners and the equally
detested Bantu. They considered the latter a possible harbinger of a second struggle for national independence.
Despite their poverty, these farmers provided the striking
miners with the food they needed during the long months
of bitter struggle.

When Andrews and other strike leaders were arrested
and imprisoned, 10,000 strikers marched through Johannesburg in protest, carrying red flags flanked by heavily armed
Commando detachments and displaying a huge banner
with the legend: WORKERS OF THE WORLD UNITE
AND FIGHT TO KEEP SOUTH AFRICA WHITE!
This shotgun marriage between Marxism and White
supremacy was one of the slogans that had aroused Bunting's deep misgivings.

The Rising Tide of Violence

Dynamite charges were planted, presumably by the
Council of Action or the Commandos, at strategic points
in the mines and throughout the Reef. The authorities
retaliated by reinforcing some 3,000 police with 1,500
special constables, recruited from the law-abiding citizens.
The murder of non-strikers reached such proportions that

the authorities were forced to illegalize the use of Commandos as strike pickets.

The Johannesburg *Star* urged the union to let the miners vote on a proposed settlement offered by the Chamber of Mines, but this ran counter to the Communist purpose of fanning the conflict toward general strike and ultimately civil war. Andrews countered with a proposal to muzzle the press: "The Typographical Union has played into the hands of the masters all through the strike by printing the lying reports and statements of the *Star* and the *Mail*. It is time that either a rigid censorship be established over the news and comments by the printers, or that the papers be stopped altogether." Meanwhile, the Augmented Executive announced that it had decided to poll the workers on whether they wanted to continue the strike or return to their jobs. The Council of Action decided to prevent this and, at Communist instigation, a general strike was declared. Throughout the Reef, the Commandos helped to spread the strike by forcefully pulling "unwilling workers" out of bakeries, shops and factories.[10]

The Commandos prepared for armed struggle and began to assemble guns and ammunition. Then, on March 7, the accumulating electrical charge of tension and violence was released in a pogrom against the Bantu. Simultaneously, at various points on the Reef, strikers launched apparently unprovoked attacks on the Natives in the course of which some 20 were killed and many more wounded.

The Communist Party had warned the strikers insistently against indulging their taste for race riots. The Commandos also repudiated the murders. As early as January, Bunting had observed: "One of the surest weapons to defeat a White strike is to get up a 'Kaffir rising' cry. . . .

[10]Cope, *op. cit.*, p. 267.

The workers forget their own cause and rush off to shoot 'niggers'—just what the bosses want in order to keep the proletariat terrorized."[11]

Up to this point, the strikers had enjoyed the sympathy of both the South African and the British Labour Parties. The March race riots turned the tide of public opinion and the strikers were depicted in the British press as murderers. The South African Native Congress urged the Government to declare martial law as a means of ensuring the safety of the non-Whites. The Minister of Justice informed the press that the attacks by Europeans on Natives and Coloured people had been "without the slightest provocation," that their underlying purpose was "to give the impression throughout the country that a Native rising on the Rand was imminent and that the lives and property of Europeans were in danger," but that the facts of the matter were that "there was not the slightest disposition on the part of any Native to cause trouble" and that any violence by Natives against Europeans had been because the former were "trying to defend themselves."[12]

Meanwhile, the political undercurrents of the struggle were becoming increasingly clear to the nation. The Durban light infantry, composed almost entirely of men of British descent and loyal to the Empire, was dispatched to the Rand to put down what it was told was a combined Bolshevik and Afrikaner republican plot to overthrow the Government.

On March 8, the Commando "generals" held a joint council of war with the Communists, but the two groups were unable to agree either on immediate measures or on

[11]*Ibid.*, p. 269.
[12]Quoted by Roux, *op. cit.*, p. 53.

fundamental aims. The Commandos then held a private meeting, from which the Communists were excluded, to plan armed resistance. The rebels seized the Johannesburg Town Hall and displayed the red flag from its roof. Under the Council of Action slogan of "the bare-armed fighting man," the strikers seized most of the Rand, occupied all of Johannesburg except a few strongpoints in which the police were entrenched, and burned the premises of the *Star* because its reporting and editorials were not to their liking.

Smuts had pursued a waiting policy, realizing the risks it entailed, but determined to educate the country to the dangers inherent in the Communist movement. He told his Cabinet on February 17 that "if we are continually walking on the edge of a volcano, let the country see it; let us, at the risk of a couple of days revolution in Johannesburg, delay the declaration of martial law and let the situation develop."

On March 8, however, he called up the police, mobilized an effective civilian force and proclaimed martial law. "This morning," he declared, "from one side of the Reef to the other, the Commandos attacked and fighting has been going on over a large part of the Rand, and is still going on, and there have been heavy casualties. . . . All essential services have been brought to a standstill, and the Natives are, from one end of the Reef to the other, in a state of turmoil. . . ."[13]

With his usual contempt for danger, Smuts took command of the troops and drove through Commando lines under heavy fire, which his friend and companion, Louis Esselen, returned, shouting, "Shoot, Oom Jannie,[14] shoot!"

[13]J. C. Smuts, *op. cit.*, pp. 229–30.
[14]"Uncle Jan."

Smuts ignored the request. A few minutes later, he asked Esselen how many bullets he had left. None. "A fine fix we might now be in," Smuts retorted, "if I had also used up all my ammunition."[15]

By now, the South African press was thoroughly alive to the danger through which the country was passing. Lurid headlines added fuel to the fears and hatreds of the citizens. Examples were: "Terrors of Red Occupation—Country Saved from Terrible Peril and Bloodshed—One of the Worst Chapters of Red Terror—Murder at Brakpan —A Mormon Town[16]—A House of the Dead—Looting under the White Flag—Nightmare of Tortured Limbs— Lenin's Last Desperate Attempt."[17]

On March 12, there was heavy fighting in the course of which 1,500 Rand rebels were captured and air bombing decimated the strikers' ranks. The Commandos retaliated by burning down houses. As dusk fell, most of the city, including the Rand ridges, had been cleared of the hostile force.[18]

On the following day, another 2,200 strikers, many of whom "wear red rosettes and frankly admitted that their aims are Bolshevist," were captured. On March 15, Commandos dynamited the railroad lines, but the Brakpan police garrison was relieved after three days without food or water. Another 4,000 prisoners were taken and the Rand Rebellion was over.

On March 22, the *New York Times* reported: "Smuts Says Rebel Aim Was a Soviet Republic."[19] He declared

[15]J. C. Smuts, *op. cit.*, p. 230.
[16]The allusion was to polygamy.
[17]Cope, *op. cit.*, p. 281. Actually, Lenin and the Communist International were not involved in these events and had little interest in South Africa.
[18]*New York Times*, March 13, 1922.
[19]*Ibid.*, March 22, 1922.

that the country had "escaped a tremendous danger, the gravity of which has not been sufficiently made clear." Smuts castigated the Mine Workers Union for not having broken with the Communists. He said that his great fear had been that "the rebels would be able to set up a revolutionary Government and mete out executions, with the result that there would be a blood bath at Johannesburg . . . comparable to the French Revolution."

Special courts charged nearly a thousand South Africans with murder, high treason and lesser crimes. Eighteen were sentenced to death and hundreds to prison. The two radical Commando leaders, Fischer and Spendiff, committed suicide rather than suffer capture. The Hanekom brothers were caught sniping and shot. A Commando called Stassen was sentenced to death and hanged for murdering two Natives, a retribution which enraged hard-core Afrikaners. The strength of Communist influence in the rising was illustrated by the fact that some of those hanged went to the gallows singing "The Red Flag" and one shouted, "Workers of the World Unite!" as the trap was dropped beneath his feet.

A parliamentary commission of inquiry revealed that the leadership of the Nationalist Party had been "deeply implicated" and had hoped to turn the strike "into something akin to a rebellion with (Orange) Free State and Western Transvaal burghers coming to assist the strikers."[20] In Parliament, General Hertzog, who had carefully avoided any disloyal involvement, reviled Smuts. "The Prime Minister's footsteps drip with blood," he told the House. "His footsteps will go down in history in this manner." During three days of derision and denunciation by Nationalist Party spokesmen, Smuts sat silently listening. At the end

[20] J. C. Smuts, *op. cit.*, p. 232.

of the debates, South African labor had been alienated from the Unionists and the future victory of the Nationalists had been assured.[21]

Bunting was arrested and held in prison, but soon released without a charge. Andrews was accused of public violence, but acquitted. The debacle of the so-called Johannesburg Soviet sent hundreds of Communists and revolutionaries into hiding. The Party headquarters was raided by the police and *The International* had to suspend publication for two months. Reds were expelled *en masse* from the trade unions and the Party went underground. When *The International* resumed publication in May 1922, Andrews wrote that the workers of South Africa were "writhing under the iron heel of a temporarily triumphant White terror."

There were the customary Communist predictions of future victory, but these did not seem in any way warranted by the objective situation. The Party organization was shattered; its membership was dwindling; it had lost its influence over the White working class of South Africa, an influence that it has not yet regained; even more important, it had made itself hated and feared as an instrument of rebellion and treason by a large majority of the White population of the country. Seemingly, the Communist Party had performed the remarkable feat of attempting an armed uprising during the second year of its existence only to sink into a gradual and protracted sickness and decline.

[21]*Ibid.*, pp. 232–33.

✧ ✧ ✧ ✧ ✧

CHAPTER FIVE

"Lord Bunting, the Imperialist Bloodsucker"

"Those who know do not speak;
"Those who speak do not know.
"Block the passages,
"Shut the doors,
"Let all sharpness be blunted,
"All tangles untied,
"All glare tempered,
"All dust smoothed.
"This is called the mysterious levelling."

—Lao Tzū, *Tao Tê Ching* (Arthur Waley
translation)

WITH THE REVOLUTIONARY TIDE RECEDING IN EUROPE, THE Communist International instructed its member parties to seek affiliation with the mass organizations of Socialist workers in their countries. Accordingly, at its Second Congress in April 1922, the South African Communist Party requested permission to merge with the Labour Party. By a decisive majority, the Labour Party rejected this proposal and shortly thereafter the Miners' Federation voted eight to one against affiliating with the Red International of Labor Unions.

In the winter of 1922, Bunting and Andrews went to Moscow to attend the Fourth Congress of the Communist International. Bunting saw the seedy and impoverished Soviet capital through ideologically tinted spectacles. He listened with apparent equanimity to a 7½-hour-long oration by Leon Trotsky and discovered that the members of the Soviet secret police had "humane and intelligent faces."[1]

The Fourth World Congress had ordered united fronts from above with the mass organizations of the workers, but this directive was resisted by more radical Communist groups throughout the world. On his return to South Africa, Bunting had to put down a Cape Town group of this sort, which disdained to support the immediate demands of labor on the grounds that these were insufficiently revolutionary.

Comintern policy called for the British Communist Party to make continuing efforts to join the Labour Party. This formula was extended to South Africa without considering the basic differences in the two situations. Adherence to the Labour Party would have forced the Communists to concentrate on the skilled White workers and largely ignore both the Black masses and the explosive issue of the color bar.

A lifelong trade unionist, Andrews energetically supported the Comintern line of affiliation at a Party conference called in Johannesburg in December 1924 to decide the matter. The opposition to affiliation was predictably led by Bunting, an intellectual with no close connections

[1]Roux, *op. cit.*, p. 58.

with the labor movement, a writer rather than a man of action, and a zealot on the race question. Edward Roux, who was closely associated with both men, summed up the clash between their personalities:

Andrews was handsome, with white hair and blue eyes, of stately appearance, reserved, careful of his dignity, a lucid and eloquent speaker, a clear and concise writer, an aristocrat of labor who had entered the Socialist movement through the trade unions. There was nothing "woolly" about him: in a crisis, he could make up his mind quickly; he had no patience with people who dithered. Bunting was dark, restless and ungainly, with the most determined jaw and big nose. He was not a natural orator. His writing was often, though not always, abstruse and involved. Anxious to do justice to all parties concerned and scrupulous in weighing all the possible consequences of any decision he might take, he seemed in a crisis over-careful and slow.[2]

In the struggle over affiliation, the Bunting, or leftwing, faction won the day. Andrews resigned as Secretary of the Communist Party and took no further part in Party activities. C. F. Glass, another Red trade union leader, resigned from the Communist Party because of its decision to concentrate on Blacks "who could not possibly appreciate the noble ideals of Communism."

South African Communism had now burned its bridges to the trade union movement and the dominant White element in labor. It was irrevocably committed to the negrophile strategy that its consumptive leader, Ivor Jones, had urged shortly before his death in the Soviet Union. "As a cold matter of fact," Jones had written Andrews, "there is not room for a C.P. in White South Africa *ex-*

[2] Roux, *op. cit.*, p. 67.

cept as a watchdog of the Native, as the promoters of *rapprochment* [sic!], watching, *within* the broader organizations, for every opportunity to switch the White movement on right lines on this question and scotching every conspiracy to rouse race hatred and strike-breaking of race against race."[3]

The Party now turned toward the Bantu and, to a lesser extent, toward the Coloured and the Indians. For several years it had boasted only one Black Party member, a certain Thibedi. The Party now proceeded to set up a night school where Bantu recruits could be taught the elements of Marxism-Leninism. Since few employers of Native labor were willing to provide them with night passes to attend a Communist school, the Party forged the necessary documents.

Meanwhile, a mass movement of African workers, called the Industrial and Commercial Workers Union of Africa (I.C.U.), was growing under the leadership of Clements Kadalie, a native of Nyasaland unfamiliar with Bantu languages, but a man of restless energy and fluency as a mass speaker. Loosely organized and modelled on the American I.W.W., Kadalie's movement launched a few big strikes in the first years of its existence, but later confined its activities to resolutions, protests and demonstrations. The I.C.U. claimed 30,000 members by September 1925, half of whom admittedly paid no dues; it would claim 100,000 some two years later.

The Communist Party penetrated the I.C.U. and tried to take control. It was opposed by prominent non-Communist White negrophiles who urged Kadalie to break with the Reds. Clashes between the Communists and the

[3]Cope, *op. cit.*, p. 296.

I.C.U. leadership concerning dues hastened Kadalie's decision, and at the 1926 annual congress of the union, Communists were given the alternative of resigning from the Party or being expelled from the I.C.U.

Faced with this ultimatum, the Communists turned toward the African National Congress, which had seemingly been eclipsed, and began to infiltrate it with their best cadres. By the 1950's and 1960's, the A.N.C. would constitute a mass movement, holding sway over hundreds of thousands of Bantu and serving as the Communist Party's main instrumentality among the Negroes. As for the I.C.U., corruption and extravagance among its leaders, a fondness for lawsuits, factional schisms and incompetent administration hastened its decline and disintegration.[4]

In July 1927, the Party emphasized its concentration on the Bantu masses by moving its headquarters from a trade union hall to a Native quarter in Johannesburg. The *South African Worker*, official organ of the Party, was transformed into a primarily Negro publication, which was printed by Bantu labor at a very large saving in wages and which published most of its articles in such Bantu tongues as Xhosa, Sotho and Zulu.

For a time, the Reds made impressive headway among the Natives. Roux recalled a meeting of 2,000 Bantu at Vereeniging at which "several hundreds joined the Party, including a number of women." At another district, the Communists clashed with the police and the Red speaker was arrested. This created such tremendous enthusiasm among the Blacks that "practically every man, woman and child in Potchefstroom location joined the C.P."[5]

[4]Cope, *op. cit.*, p. 318.
[5]Roux, *op. cit.*, pp. 79–80

Stalin and the Bantu Republic

Prior to 1927, the Comintern showed practically no interest in South Africa and neither issued directives to the Party nor sent it plenipotentiary representatives.[6] In that year, the situation changed and the Party soon found itself overwhelmed with guiding slogans, criticisms and directives, which corresponded more to Russian political requirements than to South African conditions.

In Roux's opinion, the change that occurred in 1927 was due to a Soviet belief that Great Britain was the guiding spirit behind the cordon of armed Balko-Danubian states that shielded Western Europe from Russia. To this end, Roux asserts, the Comintern decided to organize "liberation movements" among the Native populations of Britain's Empire.[7]

Actually, it is doubtful that Stalin took the Comintern's pronouncements about an impending imperialist war too seriously.[8] His opinion of the Comintern was very low and he referred to it on at least two occasions as a *Lavotchka*, or grocery store.[9]

In 1927 and 1928, the world Communist movement suffered two major international defeats: the failure of the British General Strike to develop into a revolutionary movement and the extermination of Chinese Communist forces by Generalissimo Chiang Kai-shek. Leftwing criticism of the putatively opportunistic policies of Stalin in both these situations was rife in the Communist Interna-

[6]In 1924, however, the Young Communist International, with headquarters in Berlin, ordered the South African Young Communist League to stop holding racially segregated meetings.
[7]*Ibid.*, p. 87.
[8]Guenther Nollau, *op. cit.*, p. 107.
[9]Franz Borkenau, *European Communism*. London: Faber, 1953, p. 61.

tional. Fresh from a triumph over his domestic enemies, Stalin determined to steal their thunder in the Comintern by driving it along a leftwing course. This decision may have been accentuated by the growing isolation of the Communists from the masses of European labor and would receive further impetus with the 1929 world economic crisis and the coming of the Great Depression.

After his victory over both right and left opposition groups within the Soviet Union, Stalin proceeded to transform the Communist International into a monolithic organization, centrally directed and brooking no dissent, as he had previously so transformed the Communist Party of the Soviet Union. As early as the Fifth World Congress of the Comintern (June–July 1924), the principles of "democratic centralism" and "iron Bolshevik Party discipline" had been enunciated as applicable to member Parties. South Africa's remoteness, her comparative insignificance in Comintern plans for world revolution and the defects of Comintern organization and control gave her a respite of several years from iron centralization.

The swing toward the left affected the South African Party primarily in the form of a Comintern demand for an independent Black republic to be carved out of South African territory. The impetus for this "solution" to the Negro problem came from Stalin personally. Toward the end of 1925, a Ghanese and four American Negro Communists were brought to Moscow to be trained as professional revolutionaries in the University of Toilers of the East. Within a week of their arrival, as one of the American students later reminisced,[10] Stalin sent for them and talked to them informally for several hours. He said that, since the Negroes were the most oppressed element in the

[10]Otto Hall.

American population, the Communist Party of the United
States should have more Negro than White members. Yet
it had few. The reason for this, Stalin added, was that "the
whole approach of the American Party to the Negro question is wrong. You are a national minority with some of
the characteristics of a nation."[11] The Negroes present
reacted unfavorably to this approach as it seemed to them
to smack of enforced race segregation.

On at least two other occasions, Stalin broached the
idea that the Comintern should view the American Negroes as an oppressed national minority. In advancing this
thesis, he spoke with even more than his usual authority,
since he was regarded as the Soviet Union's chief specialist
on national questions. Early in 1928, in preparation for the
Sixth World Congress of the Comintern, a subcommittee
of the Anglo-American Secretariat was set up to formulate
a resolution on the Negro question that would reflect
Stalin's wishes.

By this time, Stalin had probably committed the Communist International to the line of self-determination in
the American Black Belt, that is to say, the right of the
Negroes in a band of contiguous counties in the cotton
belt to secede from the United States and form their own
republic. South Africa was considered merely a corollary
of the United States in this respect and the tribally organized Bantu were automatically equated to the detribalized
descendants of slaves in the agrarian South.

There had been one or two anticipatory warnings. La
Guma, a South African Negro Communist, had been sent
to the Soviet Union in 1927 and had had a long conference
with Bukharin in which both agreed that the Bantus were

[11]Theodore Draper, *American Communism and the Soviet Union.* New
York: Viking Press, 1960, pp. 332–34.

the victims of national oppression. They concluded that the fundamental task of the South African Party was to shatter the imperialist rule of Briton and Boer and to substitute a "democratic, independent Native republic (which would give the White workers and other non-exploiting Whites certain 'minority rights') as a stage toward the final overthrow of capitalism in South Africa."[12]

A draft resolution embodying these thoughts was sent out to member parties by the Communist International. The Buntings and Edward Roux were chosen as delegates to the Sixth World Congress of the Comintern by the majority of the South African Communist Party and were instructed to oppose the draft resolution. Arriving in Moscow, the South Africans were snubbed by James Ford, a prominent American Negro Communist, as "White chauvinists."

Comintern policy toward the Native races was assigned to the Anglo-American Secretariat, which also had jurisdiction over Black Africa. The head of the Secretariat, who called himself A. J. Bennet, was a 100 per cent Stalin man and, in Bunting's opinion, "a slimy fellow." Bunting soon discovered that Bennet also operated under the name Petrovsky. Bennet-Petrovsky was in reality a certain Dr. Max Goldfarb, who had been labor editor of the Jewish Daily Forward in New York City and who had taken part in the vituperative factional fights of the Jewish section of the American Socialist Party. He had gone to Russia, shed Menshevism for Bolshevism and served as Comintern representative to the British Communist Party. Like many converts, Bennet-Petrovsky-Goldfarb was more orthodox than the Pope.

Bunting questioned, not only the self-determination pro-

[12]Quoted from Roux's summary, *op. cit.*, p. 89.

gram for the Bantu, but Stalin's basic conception of a revolutionary alliance between the industrial workers in the advanced countries and the "masses" in the colonial world. In South Africa, he pointed out, hundreds of thousands of Bantu were not merely "masses," but workers in the nation's industries and mines, many of them organized in militant trade unions. He rebutted the charge of "White chauvinism" by pointing out that 1,600 of the South African Communist Party's members were Natives and only 150 of them Whites. There had been only 200 non-White Party members the year before.

As the Party's most uncompromising negrophile, Bunting opposed the slogan of a "Native republic" more on tactical grounds than on those of principle. In his speech to the Congress of August 20, 1928, he said that he was defending the White workers, not because of "any special love for the aristocrats of labor or any chauvinistic preference for the Whites, as is superficially and malignantly suggested in the draft resolution," but primarily as a tactic for advancing the Native movement. "Our infant Native movement, any revolutionary Native movement, lives and moves in a perpetual state bordering on illegality; on the slightest pretext, it can be suppressed either by prosecution or legislation or by massacre or pogrom. We are therefore always looking for allies, or rather for shields and protections behind which to carry on; and even the *bare neutrality*, much more the occasional support of the White trade unions, etc., is of incalculable value to us. . . ."[13]

However, the matter had already been decided and Bunting's able speech was wasted breath. When he predicted that the new slogan would alienate the White South African working class, he was accused of "social fascism."

[13]Roux, *op. cit.*, p. 97.

In their naïveté, the Buntings were convinced that their defeat in the Comintern was due to the intrigues of underlings and that the problem was to get the ear of the real leaders of the Soviet Union and explain the South African problem to them. Nevertheless, as loyal Communists, they bowed to the decision of the World Congress and agreed to promulgate the new demand for "a South African Native Republic, as a stage toward a Workers' and Peasants' Government with full protection and equal rights for all minorities."

Sympathy from Professionals

Back in South Africa, Bunting found that, while White labor strongly opposed the Communists, they were winning sympathy from an unexpected source. A lawyer said: "A lot of us would be with you if you were not a Communist and in tow with Moscow." An Episcopalian priest exclaimed enthusiastically: "That's the stuff we ought to be preaching at St. Mary's."[14] The Party was getting support from a sector of the South African population which would continue to furnish it with recruits, financial aid, fellow travellers, dupes and civil liberties champions for the next three and a half decades. This sector comprised intellectuals, professionals and even businessmen who, for one reason or another, felt alienated from their own society and their own race. These supporters were almost always of British or Jewish stock and hardly ever of Afrikaner background. They were generally men and women with a poignant sense of the shortcomings and misdeeds of their class or race. Beginning with compassion for the non-Whites, many easily made the transition to admiration of

[14]*Ibid.*, p. 103.

the tribal African as a revolutionary force destined to destroy White society.

The leadership of the Party now included a young Englishman, Douglas Wolton, who had joined in Cape Town in 1925, and his wife, Molly Zelikowitz, a brilliant and emotional mass orator. The Woltons were leftists by temperament and also rigidly orthodox followers of Moscow. At one point, they almost left South Africa because the Communist Party refused to accede to their demand that *all* its officeholders be Blacks.

The main Negro organizations—the African National Congress and the I.C.U.—refused to endorse Moscow's demand for a Native republic. Bunting explained away the slogan as meaning simply majority rule and seemed to be weathering the storm. By January 1929, Party membership had almost doubled to reach a claimed 3,000, but the movement had become almost exclusively one of Natives who were politically ignorant and with little education or influence.

In the summer of 1929, Bunting took the lead in organizing a League of African Rights, a mass organization to fight for abolition of the pass laws, universal free education and the franchise for Natives. The League caught on like wildfire until a telegram came from Moscow ordering that it be disbanded. The explanatory letter that followed denounced the League as a reformist, rather than a revolutionary organization. After the League was scuttled, the Party again turned to the African National Congress and, behind its facade, started campaigns to get the Bantu to burn their passes and invite arrest.

The Communists had also played a leading role in building trade unions of Natives. By the end of 1928, the

Non-European Trade Union Federation boasted 10,000 members in the Rand. In his efforts to build a primarily Black Communist movement, Bunting campaigned, despite strenuous police harassment, in the tribal areas of the Transkei. Party spokesmen went to the Bantu locations to urge the populace to refuse to pay taxes. These and similar measures resulted in the creation of what was probably the strongest Negro Communist movement in the world.

The Mirage of Imminent Revolution

Isolated from the organized labor movement of Europe and America, the Comintern committed itself to an ultra-leftwing course. The Party leaderships in Germany, the United States and other countries were accused of right-wing opportunism and expelled. Bukharin was ousted from the Politburo of the Soviet Party on the same grounds, thus removing the last substantial barrier to the complete Stalinization of the world Communist movement.

The Tenth Plenum of the Executive Committee of the Communist International (E.C.C.I.), meeting in Moscow in 1929, proclaimed the new leftist political line. The Socialists were branded as "social fascists," as "the party that betrays and murders the working class."[15] Revolutionary Socialists were the most dangerous of the deceivers of the proletariat—"the more to the left, the more dangerous."[16]

The economic crisis of the fall of 1929 had become a world depression of intensifying gravity. The Comintern triumphantly proclaimed that it had predicted this catastro-

[15]Resolution of the 12th Congress of the German Communist Party (K.P.D.).
[16]Quoted by Isaac Deutscher, *Stalin*. New York: Oxford University Press, 1949, p. 405.

phe with its infallible analytic tool, Marxism-Leninism. And so it had: it had been predicting world economic crisis continuously during the entire era of prosperity!

At the Tenth Plenum, the Comintern proclaimed that the world had entered into a Third Period, which marked the end of the post–World War I era of capitalist stabilization and ushered in a new round of wars and revolutions that would end with the global victory of Communism. This assertion that the subjective conditions for social revolution were ripe or on the verge of ripening was a ghastly misreading of history, for the decade ahead would be characterized by the worldwide advance of Nazism and the disorganized retreat of Communist and Socialist forces. From this faulty vision of the impending course of events, the Comintern inferred that all leftwing, non-Communist movements (except those controlled by Moscow) must be unmasked as capitalist schemes to betray the working class and deflect it from its revolutionary mission; that the Socialists must be continuously exposed as agents of capitalism, betrayers of labor and allies of fascism; that the Communists must advance purely revolutionary demands; that the Parties must go to the masses openly as Communist organizations; and, most important of all, that they must make practical preparations for proletarian insurrection and the establishment of Soviet power.

This leftist orientation either destroyed the Communist Parties or radically transformed their membership. In industrial countries, such as Germany, they became primarily organizations of the unemployed, a desperate flotsam of society made even more desperate by depression, and of extremist intellectuals. The Communists lost most of what they had previously won in the trade unions and the ranks of skilled labor. In South Africa, the application of these policies meant that the Communist Party lost its foothold in the White labor movement, but attracted intellectuals, semi-intellectuals, the unemployed, the unskilled and discontented people without strong social roots.

The Campaign Against Bunting

Wolton went to Moscow for indoctrination in the new strategy and tactics, returning to South Africa in November 1930 armed with Comintern directives that denounced Bunting and Roux as White chauvinists and social reformers. Wolton then took over Bunting's post as General Secretary of the Communist Party.

The campaign against Bunting rapidly gathered momentum. He was accused of such crimes as "the removal of Native functionaries from the leadership of the Party," which meant specifically that he had had a man named Nzula ousted from his Party post when the latter repeatedly arrived at meetings drunk. Bunting replied to these charges in a letter that was published in the official Party organ, *Umzebenzi* (meaning *The Worker* in Xhosa). Douglas Wolton and a brilliant Lithuanian Jew named Lazar Bach, who now ran the Party unchallenged, "sharply condemned" *Umzebenzi* for publishing Bunting's side of the story. *Umzebenzi* was transformed into a ponderous doctrinal publication, written in an unreadable and verbose style and more calculated to appeal to Moscow higher-ups than to South African workers. Wolton acquired the nickname among Native Communists of "Deepening Economic Crisis," because his articles generally began with an allusion to this phenomenon.[17]

The Party did have some successes. In May 1930, Izzy

[17]Roux, *op. cit.*, p. 128.

Diamond led a big demonstration of unemployed demanding bread, which was remarkable because it was interracial. For this, he received a year in prison, and Molly Wolton became the main agitator among and organizer of the jobless. Communist demonstrations of the unemployed invariably included both Whites and Blacks. However, most of the White jobless were Afrikaners and, in consequence, the marches and protests might start with approximately equal numbers of the two races, but would end almost entirely Negro.[18]

Believing the Comintern predictions that the proletarian insurrection was just around the corner, Bach and the Woltons consistently remained in the background and let the non-White Party activists take all the risks. They apparently considered that, as the brains of the coming revolution, they had no right to expose themselves unnecessarily to danger. To such leaders as Bunting and the mass agitator, Izzy Diamond, however, they seemed to be simply cowards.

In September 1931, Wolton and Bach finally made a clean sweep of the men who had built the South African Communist Party. The two founders, Bunting and Andrews, were expelled on paltry charges. Almost equally serious for the future of the movement was the expulsion of key trade union leaders, primarily of the non-Whites, such as Sollie Sachs, Secretary of the Garment Workers' Union, Benny Weinbren, President of the Native Trade Union Federation, and C. B. Tyler, Secretary of the Building Workers' Industrial Union.

The expulsion of these and other trade union leaders virtually destroyed the labor organizations of Natives, to the

---

[18]Edward Roux, *Time Longer Than Rope*. Madison: University of Wisconsin Press, 2nd edition, 1964, p. 269.

creation of which the Party had devoted so much effort. The expelled leaders were not permitted to continue to run their unions, but were subjected to incessant vilification and intrigue until these labor groups disintegrated into factions.

The Communists soon lost most of the ground they had gained among the Natives. Pursuing the policy dictated by Moscow, they denounced virtually all Bantu leaders who were not either Communists or docile tools of the Party as reformists, lackeys of capitalism and Uncle Toms. These tirades aroused widespread distrust of the Communists and split and demoralized the movements they sought to control.

The Communist Party, which had claimed 3,000 members in 1929, shrank to probably no more than 150, of whom the majority were White. There were branches at Johannesburg and Cape Town, some underground organizations in Natal and two other active branches in the Eastern Cape Province.[19] Nothing else was left.

Making the same mistake that he had made in Moscow in 1928, Bunting laid his expulsion at the door of Wolton and the Party bureaucracy. He refused to recognize that Wolton and Bach were mere instruments of Moscow policy.

Meanwhile, the campaign against him intensified. When Bunting called a meeting of his supporters, the Party got the Jewish Workers' Club, consisting of fanatically orthodox Communists, to hold a meeting at the same place and time ostensibly to protest police brutality. Bunting's followers protested the intrusion and a fight broke out. The next issue of *Umzebenzi* carried the headline: "BUNTINGITES SMASH UP IKAKA CONFERENCE, Agents

[19]*Ibid.*, p. 269.

of Pirow and Hertzog Prevent Exposure of Prison Brutalities." The paper charged Bunting with organizing "groups of renegade Communists and others in order to prevent the delegates from speaking of the prison conditions which they had experienced" and concluded that this proved conclusively that Bunting had become "a definite agent of the Government. . . ."[20] Unable to understand or cope with methods of this sort, Bunting had a stroke. When he recovered partially, he gave up active politics and became a viola player.

The fact that thousands of ill-trained and politically ignorant Negroes left the Party during the Third Period was not entirely calamitous. Lenin and Stalin had never viewed the Communist Party as a horde of emotional rebels, but rather as a disciplined, elite organization of professional revolutionaries "armed with revolutionary theory . . . with a knowledge of the laws of revolution."[21] The backward Bantu communities that had joined the Communist Party in droves in the late 1920's and early 1930's as an emotional protest against the authorities were more the stuff of revivalist meetings than of revolution. Although many Natives were laboriously indoctrinated in Party night schools in the fundamentals of Marxism-Leninism, even such a politically orthodox Communist as Cope considered them untrained, undisciplined and unable to withstand pressure.[22] One Bantu Communist identified the Party so completely with Bunting that he observed that it wore big boots. In an effort to develop the capabilities of Bantu Communists and train them for national leadership,

[20]Roux, *S. P. Bunting*, p. 139.
[21]Joseph Stalin, Lecture delivered at Sverdlov University in April 1924. A *Handbook of Marxism*. New York: International Publishers, 1935, pp. 940–41.
[22]Cope, *op. cit.*, p. 325.

Nzula was sent to the Lenin School in Moscow, at the time the most important advanced academy for professional revolutionaries in the world. Nzula, however, got drunk, fell asleep in the Russian snow and died of pneumonia.

In 1932, the Party began to go underground. Its thinned ranks were further diluted by assigning some of its few remaining members the task of setting up a shadow organization. These members were, of course, forbidden to engage in any open Party work since that would have exposed them to the attention of the police and jeopardized the secrecy of their illegal organization. Harassed and weakened as it was, the Party found time to attack "Lord Bunting, the imperialist bloodsucker."[23]

In 1933, Wolton served a sentence of three months' hard labor for inciting to riot, following a previous term for criminal defamation. He emerged in a depressed state, harassed, his wife suffering from heart trouble and their daughter disturbed by being deprived of a normal family life. Offered a job on an English newspaper by his brother, Wolton left the country without requesting permission from the Comintern representative.[24] There was irony in the fact that this man, who had been so uncompromising and inhuman in driving others in the name of the Party, should have deserted his post.

After the departure of the Woltons, the fight against "right opportunism" continued for a while, and, under Lazar Bach's inflexible rule, the Party ousted Roux and Moses Kotane, an able Bantu, from leadership. When Moscow inaugurated the new popular front policy, Bach

[23]Bunting's father, a scholar and musician, had been knighted.
[24]The Comintern had a resident representative in South Africa at the time, but available documents do not identify him.

was summoned to Moscow to answer questions concerning his leadership of the South African Party. In Russia, this guardian of Stalinist orthodoxy became acquainted with a man who was later purged as a Trotskyite. For having failed to inform the N.K.V.D. of the latter's political shortcomings, Bach fell victim to the great purge and was probably shot.

❖ ❖ ❖ ❖ ❖

CHAPTER SIX

Anti-Semitism
and World War

"The revolutionary enters the world of the state, of the classes
and of so-called civilization, and he lives in this world only because he has faith in its quick and complete destruction. He no
longer remains a revolutionary if he keeps faith with anything
in this world. *He should not hesitate to destroy any position, any
place or any man in this world.* He must hate everything and
everyone with an equal hatred. All the worse for him if he has
in the world relationships with parents, friends, or lovers; *he is no
longer a revolutionary if he is swayed by these relationships.*"

—Sergei Gennadiyevich Nechayev,
The Revolutionary Catechism[1]

Meeting in Moscow in 1935, the Seventh World Congress of the Communist International responded to the
advance of Nazism by abolishing the Third Period strategy
and substituting that of the Popular Front. The central
objective of all Communist Parties became the destruction
of fascism and to this end every effort was made to estab-

---

[1]Translated by Robert Payne. From *Zero*, New York: John Day, 1950,
pp. 10–11. Emphasis in the original.

lish united fronts with Socialist, labor, progressive and liberal organizations. The Communists were directed to support anti-Nazi movements and coalitions everywhere. To make themselves more acceptable to their would-be allies and dupes, they were to soft-pedal their revolutionary ideology and represent themselves as fervent advocates of democracy.

This violent *volte face* corresponded to and was dictated by the desperate emerging crisis in Soviet foreign policy. Stalin had made an almost fatal misjudgment of the power, durability and purposes of Nazism. He had apparently convinced himself that Hitler's regime would be advantageous to the Soviet Union. Thus, a year after the Nazis took power, Stalin assured the 17th Congress of the Communist Party of the Soviet Union (C.P.S.U.) that "the revolutionary crisis is maturing and fascism is far from being long-lived."[2] Somewhat later, he told the German Communist leader, Heinz Neumann, that the Nazi regime would become so embroiled with aggression in Western Europe that Russia "would be able to build up Socialism undisturbed."[3] Stalin at first attempted cooperation with Hitler and it was only in 1934, when the German dictator ordered the Reichswehr to cease all joint activities with the Red Army, that Stalin began to suspect that the primary Nazi drive for conquest might be directed against the Soviet Union. The complete change in Comintern policy was proclaimed at the Seventh World Congress a year later and the Communist Parties of all nations were compelled to switch instantly to popular front strategy and tactics.

[2]V. Deutscher, *op. cit.*, p. 407.
[3]Margarete Buber-Neumann, *Potsdam-Moskau*, p. 284. Cited by Nollau, *op. cit.*, p. 113.

In South Africa, such extreme negrophile Communists as Edward Roux broke with the Party on the grounds that the new direction was excessively conciliatory toward capitalism and toward the segregationist regime in Pretoria. These leftwingers realized that the new Trojan Horse approach to the Free World precluded stirring up the Negro masses and propagandizing them for insurrection and race war.

Communists and Clergy

The new line made reappraisal of the potential role of the Christian churches necessary. As early as 1933, the South African Communist leaders had realized that anti-religious propaganda merely antagonized and alienated the Bantu. They now began to see that the missionaries and ministers "were in many ways the natural allies of the Communists," particularly where the race issue was involved, and that, on certain issues, they could "make a united front with some of the parsons."[4]

Thus, a pattern of cooperation between the Communists and the anti-segregationist elements in the South African clergy began to take shape. As the years passed, ministerial support for Communist and Communist-front activities would play a major role in South African leftwing politics and the incessant clerical denunciations of the South African Government would prove to be one of the main forces that turned world opinion against it.

The Methodists, Congregationalists and Catholics were most prone to elect or appoint non-White ecclesiastics, but it was the Anglicans who took the leadership in political opposition to the regime and to its Apartheid and

[4]Edward Roux, *Time Longer Than Rope*, p. 277.

color-bar legislation.[5] The Dutch Reformed Church, which exerted and continues to exert enormous spiritual influence over the Afrikaner people and which adheres to Calvinist doctrines of elitism, remained a bulwark of the South African social order and, despite a few powerful voices of dissent from within its clergy, consistently supported racial segregation.

The nexus between the "liberal" clergymen and the Communist Party varied from sympathetic aid to outright membership. An interesting case was that of the Reverend Michael Scott, an Anglican priest who was to be prominent for a quarter of a century in every protest movement against South African oppression of Natives, real or imagined, and who was to be characterized in Eric A. Walker's history as a "saintly Anglican clergyman."[6] Definitions of sanctity will no doubt vary widely, but it is generally considered incompatible with use of a priestly office as camouflage for clandestine, illegal activities in support of an atheist movement. Yet Dr. Scott revealed in his autobiography, A Time to Speak, that he had operated for years as an international courier for underground Communist Parties and as a Comintern paymaster for illegal Red apparatuses and their agents. The Nazi-Soviet Pact of 1939 so shocked Dr. Scott that he briefly enlisted in the Royal Air Force. Discharged from it, Scott turned up in South Africa in 1940 where he immediately "made contact with some of the South African Communists" despite the fact that the Nazi-Soviet Pact was still operative and the South African Communist Party was doing its utmost to sabotage the war effort of the Western democracies.[7]

[5]Douglas Brown, Against the World. London: Collins, 1966, pp. 181–82.
[6]Walker, op. cit., p. 790.
[7]Michael Scott, A Time to Speak. London: Faber & Faber, 1958; Harold Soref and Ian Greig, The Puppeteers. London: Tandem, 1965, p. 103.

Anti-Semitism and pro-Nazi Activities

When Jan Hofmeyr, the liberal South African political leader, returned from a diplomatic mission in India to his native land in 1936, he found that anti-Semitic and pro-Nazi movements were raging. For political reasons, Daniel François Malan, leader of the Nationalist Party, demanded that Jewish immigration into South Africa be banned on the theory that the Jews were unassimilable.[8] He went beyond this and praised the Grey Shirts,[9] an organization that, though professedly non-political, was both anti-Semitic and pro-Hitler.[10]

Among Germans and South Africans of German descent, branches of such avowedly Nazi organizations as the *Hitler Jugend*, the *Arbeitsfront* and *Kraft durch Freude* were organized on South African soil.[11] More dangerous were the movements that had no open connection with Nazi Germany, that claimed to be nationalist in character, but were, to a greater or lesser extent, echoes of Nazism. Pro-Nazi- and anti–Semitic organizations of this character included the Grey Shirts, Brown Shirts and Black Shirts, the New Order and the *Ossewa-Brandwag* (O.B.). This last was the most important and the largest. Organized as a nationalist Afrikaner movement based on the heritage of the successive treks into the interior to escape British domination, the *Ossewa-Brandwag* (literally Ox-Wagon Fire Guard) claimed a membership of over 200,000 by 1940. It soon

[8]Although he was the most leftwing figure in the South African Government, Hofmeyr had himself previously approved restrictions on Jewish immigration.
[9]Alan Paton, *South African Tragedy*. New York: Scribner's, 1966, p. 193.
[10]William Henry Vatcher, Jr., *White Laager*. London: Pall Mall Press, 1965, p. 64.
[11]Hitler Youth, Labor Front and Strength through Joy.

declared that its primary purpose was to create a Christian Nationalist Republic, organized its own Storm Troops (*Sturmjaers*), probably using the swastika as one of its emblems, and forbade its members to do business with "the man with the crooked nose, the danger to the country."[12]

The growing anti-Jewish stance of Dr. Malan was ominous, for Malan was by no means an extremist. He represented the Nationalist Party in Cape Province and the Cape Afrikaners were the moderates, the descendants of those people of Dutch descent who had remained where they were under British rule and prospered. The extremists and diehards were to be found mostly among the Nationalists of the Transvaal and Orange Free State, men whose ancestors had taken part in the various treks into the hinterland to escape the authority of the Crown and to assert their right to handle their "kaffirs" as they saw fit. Moreover, Malan was a scholar who had taken his doctorate in philosophy at a Netherlands university with a thesis on Bishop Berkeley. Yet by 1937, Malan was lumping Jews and non-Whites together and accusing Hofmeyr of being their spokesman. "We want in South Africa a strong Nordic front of English- and Afrikaans-speaking people," he proclaimed.[13]

For the most part, the Jews had come to South Africa from Lithuania at the turn of the century as refugees from Czarist oppression and state-instigated pogroms. Arriving with little or no property, they began often as peddlers, carrying their packs of wares from one Afrikaner *dorp* to another and bringing the manufactured goods of the cities to isolated hinterland settlements. They had been popular at first, but, by the mid-1930's, this was no longer the

[12]Vatcher, *op. cit.*, pp. 65–66.
[13]Paton, *op. cit.*, p. 201.

case. The Jews had become heavily urbanized. In Johannesburg, they constituted 17 per cent of the population and were sufficiently conspicuous so that the metropolis was sometimes referred to, not as Jo'burg, but as Jewburg. They aroused envy and some rancor during the years of depression because they controlled a large part of the business of Johannesburg and other cities.[14]

Support for the Nazis derived from a variety of factors. Among these was the high proportion of German blood in the White population of South Africa, hatred of England as the traditional enemy of Afrikaner nationalism and strong sympathy for Hitler's view that the Negro was not only inferior, but an element that would contaminate White civilization unless quarantined from it. Anti-Semitism was fed by the economic discontent of the Afrikaner poor Whites, both rural and urban. A perhaps more important ingredient was the prominence of South African Jews in finance, mining and the other economic command posts of the nation, on the one hand, and in revolutionary and racial reform movements, on the other. From the outset, the Jews had been prominent in the Communist Party and its various fronts. They were equally conspicuous in the various movements which sought to break down the barriers separating the White from the non-White population. South African anti-Semitic propaganda, accordingly, followed the Nazi model and depicted the Jew as a deracinated element who sought to destroy White civilization and nationalism with the twin weapons of Communism and international finance. Given the visible prominence of Jews in both areas, this doctrine often fell on receptive ears.

In 1936, some 500 Jewish refugees from Nazi oppression

[14]Walker, op. cit., p. 655.

managed to reach Cape Town by ship before stringent immigration restrictions, backed by Malan and his Nationalists, closed the South African haven. Dr. Hendrik Verwoerd, at the time Professor of Psychology at Stellenbosch University, demanded that these unfortunate people be denied permission to land. Later, as editor of the powerful Nationalist newspaper, *Die Transvaler*, Dr. Verwoerd was accused of spreading Nazi doctrines. He brought suit for libel, but lost his case before Justice Philip Millin, husband of Sarah Gertrude Millin, the novelist. "On the evidence," the court concluded, "he is not entitled to complain. He did support Nazi propaganda, he did make his paper a tool of the Nazis in South Africa and he knew it."[15]

The Nationalists explained this verdict away as due to the fact that Justice Millin was Jewish. To the extent that it sought to reduce Verwoerd to the level of a puppet or imitator of Hitler, the verdict reflected the passions of 1943. Verwoerd never had anything to do with the Nazi movements in South Africa. According to the testimony of Bernard Sachs, an enemy of the regime and brother of the former Communist leader, Solly Sachs, Dr. Verwoerd "never attacked the Jews, so far as either Dr. Marais or I can recollect."[16]

Dr. Malan's flirtation with some of the pro-Nazi movements was designed to ensure that the latter would not compete effectively with the Nationalist Party for the support of the poor White Afrikaner masses. He reorganized the Party on a cell basis and vested supreme political authority in his own person. In both the Transvaal and

[15]Paton, *op. cit.*, p. 293.
[16]Bernard Sachs, *The Road from Sharpeville*. New York: Marzani & Munsell, 1961, p. 34. A leader of the anti-segregationist forces in the Dutch Reformed Church, Dr. Ben Marais is a former Professor of the History of Christianity at Pretoria University.

Orange Free State, he tolerated exclusion of Jews from Nationalist Party membership, measures which would later be repealed. Having established his own power position, Malan forced Oswald Pirow, leader of the New Order, to choose between propagating Nazi doctrines and remaining in the Nationalist Party. Pirow and his followers seceded, formed a splinter political group and vanished into oblivion. When South Africa entered World War II, the *Sturmjaers* of the *Ossewa-Brandwag* became implicated in the accumulation of illicit caches of arms, acts of terrorism and plans for insurrection. Smuts outlawed the *Ossewa-Brandwag* and legislation was passed punishing sabotage with life imprisonment. Thereafter, the pro-Nazi and anti-Semitic movement in South Africa slowly faded into insignificance.

Revival of the Communist Party

In the late 1930's, Moses Kotane was named General Secretary of the Communist Party. A Bantu of Bechuana parentage, he had been educated in a Lutheran mission school and recruited into the Party through trade union activity. At the age of 26, Kotane was sent to Moscow for advanced training as a professional revolutionary. Returning to South Africa in the early 1930's, he opposed the divisive policies of the Woltons and Bach and escaped expulsion from the Party only because of his race.

The Italian invasion of Ethiopia gave a brief impetus to Communist organization and propaganda since it awakened a large section of the African masses from their chronic political torpor, stimulated a rapid growth of the Bantu-language press and created a cult, the hero of which was Emperor Haile Selassie. Although the Lion of Judah had pointed out on several occasions that he was not a Negro, but a Semite of the Caucasian race, as were all the ruling Amhara in Ethiopia, the Bantu regarded him as their champion. When the Ethiopians were defeated, disillusionment among the Bantu was widespread and the Communists lost much of the ground they had captured.

South Africa entered the war by a narrow parliamentary majority, doing so primarily because of the ineptitude displayed by Hertzog in his advocacy of neutrality. Smuts emerged as the war leader of the nation. Malan and the Nationalists justified Japanese expansion and regarded Soviet Communism as the main enemy.

Echoing the new Moscow line, which reflected the Nazi-Soviet Pact that had been signed on the eve of hostilities, the Communist Party denounced the war as an imperialist struggle in the outcome of which the working class could have no interest. Natives were being recruited to serve as stretcher-bearers and laborers in the Western Desert. The Party agitated against this recruitment, telling the Blacks that they had been promised arms, but would merely be given *assegais*, and adding that the Bantu dead, after having been buried with Whites in mass graves, were then disinterred and placed in racially separate burial pits.[17] When the Government asked Roux to use his influence among the Africans to get them to enlist as laborers for the armed forces, he replied that, if the authorities would abolish the pass laws, he would think about it. Andrews, who had rejoined the Party in 1938 and been given the largely honorific post of Chairman of the Central Committee, parroted the Kremlin's anti-war line.

---

[17]Roux, *Time Longer Than Rope*, p. 307. The South African Bantu were never promised arms. The charge about reburial in segregated graves, however, was true.

In June 1941, Germany invaded the U.S.S.R. and the Communists, in South Africa as elsewhere in the world, immediately became ardent advocates of all-out war. Red propaganda against recruitment of Natives abruptly ceased. Justice Minister Dr. Colin Steyn released White Communists, who had been interned for suspected disloyalty, and when Moses Kotane was arrested, intervention with the authorities secured his release. Censorship was lifted on the Party's publications in English, but retained in the case of *Inkululeko (Freedom)*, which had replaced *Umzebenzi (The Worker)* as the Communist Bantu-language organ. The Communists were even permitted to go into the African locations and agitate against the pass laws provided they coupled this with prowar speeches.

At the end of the war, the Communist Party enjoyed considerable prestige, was treated by the Smuts Government with benevolent neutrality and profited from the immense popularity of the Soviet Union and its victorious Red Army. The war alliance between the U.S.S.R. and the Western democracies had made Communism a respectable philosophy and the Communist Party a legal and socially acceptable institution—factors of paramount importance in catalyzing a movement of South African intellectuals toward sympathy and rapport with the Soviet ideology.

Fear of South African Nazism had politicalized the Jewish population and a significant minority had either joined the Communist Party or was active in one or more of its various fellow traveller organizations. Thus, Michael Harmel, a Jewish Communist who would later become a member of the Party's Central Committee, boasted in writing to the Central Executive Committee on March 7, 1945, that the Party controlled the Jewish Board of Deputies, the central organization of South African Jewry, adding that the Red majority would be increased in the forthcoming elections.[18] On March 14, Harmel was reprimanded for indiscretion in transmitting this information by letter, and rightly so, for the note fell into the hands of the South African police.

Building the Non-White Trade Unions

During the late 1930's, the Nationalists had made a vigorous effort to oust the Communists from the leadership of trade unions and to base them on rigid segregation. Where the Communist leaders of these unions were also Jews, the struggle could become doubly bitter. A case in point was the Garment Workers' Union, which had been dominated since 1928 by Solly Sachs, a Jewish student of trade unionism with no experience as a worker. Since the needle trade workers were chiefly Afrikaner girls from the country, the Nationalists were able to build a rival union free of the Communist virus. Sachs remained in control of the parent labor organization. Throughout the war years, the Afrikaner labor force was slowly displaced by Coloured workers and bitter battles were fought between Sachs and his followers, who urged labor solidarity regardless of race, and the White workers, who habitually downed tools rather than allow the Coloured girls, whom they called *bastermeids* (half-breed or bastard girls), to work in the same factories with them.[19]

During the decade that ended with Hiroshima, the

[18]*Report of an Investigation of the Communist Party in South Africa* by Police Captain (later Colonel) D. H. Botha. Based on extensive seized or copied Communist documentation, the report was made to the Smuts Administration in 1946, but was not made public until 1952 when the Nationalists were in power and Malan was Prime Minister. The South African *Hansard* reference is pp. 8709–32, June 13, 1952. It will hereafter be referred to as *Botha Report* without pagination.
[19]For a fuller account, see Sachs, *op. cit.*, pp. 133–45.

South African Communist Party was quite successful in organizing trade unions of the non-White workers. In addition to Solly Sachs' activities, Ray Alexander, a young woman Communist, organized about a dozen unions in the Cape area, setting them up on an interracial basis. In Natal, the Reds brought Indian labor into trade unions. Under the veteran Cape Coloured Communist leader, J. B. Marks, an African Mine Workers' Union managed to enroll a few thousand of the 400,000-odd Black workers in the gold mines.[20] However, during the war years, the activities of this union were severely hampered by War Measure No. 1,425, which required a special permit before meetings of more than twenty people could be held on mine property.

The South African Communist Party stressed the crucial importance of the trade unions. It exhorted its members not to split them and form separate groups of their own, but to infiltrate the mass organizations of labor and seek to gain control over them. The Communists were also directed to fight for racial equality within the unions, for the right of non-Whites to organize and for the establishment of African unions. Unfortunately for the Party, the interracial directive was in conflict with the order to penetrate and control the mass organizations of labor since these were Afrikaner-oriented and a bulwark of race segregation.

Once Nazi Germany had been defeated, the Soviet Union no longer needed the flow of South African troops and matériel of war to the Western Front. The win-the-war-at-all-costs and popular front ideologies were swiftly dropped and, under Moscow's orders, the world Communist movement, that of South Africa included, reverted to a

[20]Roux, *Time Longer Than Rope*, pp. 330–36.

more leftist line and the old doctrine of class against class.

Accordingly, the Party decided to organize a strike of Bantu mine workers on the Reef. On April 14, 1946, the Red-controlled African Mine Workers' Union served notice on the Chamber of Mines that all Native workers would have to be paid a minimum wage of 10 shillings a day. This measure was propounded on the grounds that it corresponded to "the new world principles for an improved standard of living subscribed to by our Government" at the United Nations organizational meeting in San Francisco. Actually, the demand constituted a seven-fold increase over the prevailing wage of a shilling and sixpence and was made on the realistic assumption that there was no possibility that the mine owners might accept it. The demand was designed to precipitate and make unavoidable a savage conflict.

On May 28, the Johannesburg District Committee of the Party planned the strike action and forwarded its proposals by secret courier to Cape Town, where the Central Committee of the Party approved the blueprint.[21] The strike erupted on August 12 and involved some 50,000 African miners or approximately one out of every eight. As Prime Minister Jan Christian Smuts departed for a United Nations meeting at Lake Success, he stated in Johannesburg that the strike was not due to grievances, but was the work of agitators. Smuts turned over power in his absence to Jan Hofmeyr.

This situation fitted into the new Communist strategy of seeking to polarize South African society into irreconcilable conflicting groups and to discredit liberal leaders, such as Hofmeyr, who sought policies of compromise and accommodation. On August 14, some 4,000 Bantu miners,

[21]*Botha Report.*

armed with axes and other weapons, mobilized and began to march on Johannesburg. Disturbed at the potentialities for riot of this Communist-led movement, the White authorities threw the entire available police force of the Witwatersrand into action. Driven back into the mines, the Bantu abandoned their attempted march, leaving their wounded and dead behind them.

A month later, the police raided the offices of the Communist Party, the Springbok Legion,[22] the Red-controlled trade unions and the Communist publication, *The Guardian*, explaining that this move was not directed against Communism *per se*, but was a necessary reaction against the violence of the mine strike. There were the usual protests to be expected in such circumstances from White liberal intellectuals, and the South African political scientist, Leo Marquard, told Hofmeyr that he "deprecated" any attack on the Left.[23]

The Natives Representative Council used the mine strike as a pretext for forcing a definitive break with the Government. This largely powerless advisory body was sensitive to the mood of the African Nationalist Congress, which, under Communist leadership, was swiftly moving toward demands for full racial equality and direct action.

On November 26, the Council demanded that Hofmeyr commit himself to fundamental revision of the race legislation of South Africa. When he refused, Professor Z. K. Matthews, a Bantu intellectual of more than average ability, moved that the Council adjourn *sine die*, and this motion was carried. This liquidation of the Council marked, in Paton's opinion, "a turning-point in South African history," after which the non-Whites would cease

---

[22]The Communist-controlled veterans organization.
[23]Paton, *op. cit.*, p. 337.

to demand reform and would insist upon full political and juridical equality.[24]

Hofmeyr was full of deep forebodings at this intransigent course. Smuts warned the nascent United Nations in vain that, if it sought to interfere in the domestic institutions and internal problems of member states, it would bring about its own destruction. He, too, saw no untroubled road ahead for his country.

Even though the mine strike had been swiftly and decisively shattered and the African Mine Workers' Union had been virtually destroyed, the Communist Party had scored a major success. It had increased South Africa's isolation, sharpened the struggle and polarized positions to such an extent that the more moderate and constructive non-White leaders would find themselves driven closer and closer to the Communist camp.

[24]*Ibid.*, p. 338.

✧ ✧ ✧ ✧ ✧

CHAPTER SEVEN

Bantu Masses
Set into Motion

"Why should the people of your race be colonized, and where? . . . You and we are different races. We have between us a broader difference than exists between almost any other two races. Whether it is right or wrong I need not discuss; but this physical difference is a great disadvantage to us both, as I think. Your race suffers very greatly, many of them, by living among us, while ours suffers from your presence. . . . The aspiration of men is to enjoy equality with the best when free, but on this broad continent not a single man of your race is made the equal of a single man of ours."

—ABRAHAM LINCOLN *to a Negro delegation*
to the White House, August 14, 1862[1]

SOUTH AFRICA FACED HER FIRST POSTWAR ELECTION IN 1948. The Nationalist Party under Dr. Malan campaigned on a program of strict racial Apartheid, benefits to ex-servicemen, suppression of domestic subversive movements and active South African participation in the emerging Western anti-Communist alliance. The Nationalists pro-

[1]Carl Sandburg, *Abraham Lincoln: The War Years.* New York: Harcourt, Brace & Company, 1939. Vol. I, pp. 574–75.

posed to strike Cape Coloured voters from the general rolls and to have them represented by specially elected White deputies. At the same time, the Coloured were to be protected against competition by the stronger and more hardy Bantu. Their progressive segregation from White South Africa was to be accompanied by the creation of their own elective representative institutions. The Nationalists concentrated their arrows on Jan Hofmeyr whom they accused, probably unjustly, of desiring full political equality for non-Whites. The inevitable consequence of this, Malan's followers asserted, would be that South Africans would become "a coffee-colored race."

To the consternation and amazement of the ruling United Party, the Nationalists won the elections, taking the bulk of the rural constituencies, winning everywhere that Afrikaans was the spoken tongue, swamping their opponents in the Transvaal and even ousting Smuts from the seat which he had occupied for a quarter of a century.

The triumph of the Nationalists in 1948 has often been depicted as a strange and tragic accident of history. As the jacket blurb of Alan Paton's biography of Hofmeyr put it: "The story of South Africa today is inextricably bound to the life of Jan Hofmeyr. For Hofmeyr represented perhaps the last hope for a liberal policy in government as opposed to the present extremist policies of apartheid." Yet it is obvious to anyone reading Paton's unexpectedly objective biography that Hofmeyr was never a popular figure and that he owed his long tenure of high office to his brilliance, ability and integrity and to the political protection of Jan Christian Smuts. On broader grounds, it would seem that the liberal interpretation of the 1948 election does violence to the facts. The White majority, which has always ruled

in South Africa, was primarily Afrikaner in language, out-
look and culture; it was deeply committed to racial segregation; it consisted in large part of comparatively poor
Whites to whom the Nationalist social welfare programs
appealed.

Ever since the dawn of representative government, South
Africa has been ruled by men of Dutch descent. Smuts,
himself, the standard-bearer of the pro-Commonwealth
United Party, owed his stature among the common people
to his legendary exploits as a Boer military leader. As one
looks at the last six decades of South Africa's political
history, the trend seems unmistakably toward increasing
Afrikaner domination and toward political reversal of the
military verdict of the Anglo-Boer War. The interruption
of this trend occurred in 1939–48 when Smuts governed
the country as war leader, a position he owed to the fact
that General Hertzog, in urging South Africa to remain
neutral, had shocked his own Party by offering excuses for
Hitler and the Nazis.[2] Once in office, Smuts had been able
to maintain his position with the aid of emergency legislation and backed by a nation that faced both a foreign
enemy and an internal fifth column. When the war was
over, however, the nation reverted to its previous political
pattern and the narrow Nationalist victory of 1948 was
followed by increasingly decisive majorities in all the elections to follow.

The Jews, Israel and the Nationalists

The Nationalist victory of 1948 plunged the Jewish community "into the deepest gloom." Fearing that a pro-Nazi

[2]Walker, *op. cit.*, p. 693.

regime had taken power to persecute them, the Jews
"walked the streets in a daze."[3] South African Jews remem-
bered Nationalist opposition to Jewish immigration during
the 1930's, the barring of Jews from membership in the
Nationalist Party in the Transvaal and a 1937 statement
by the Nationalist Party Secretary praising the pro-Nazi
Grey Shirts for having "persistently drawn the attention of
the people to the Jewish problem which has indeed assumed very threatening proportions."

Once elected, Dr. Malan announced that he and his
Party opposed any discrimination within the White population and would welcome the day when there would be
no further discussion of the so-called Jewish problem. To
the amazement of South African Jewry, the Nationalist
Government was one of the first states to accord diplomatic recognition to Israel. Dr. Malan permitted South
African Jews to serve in Israel's War of Independence.
South Africa provided "the largest number of volunteers"
and they became "the nucleus of the Israel Air Force."[4]
Among the prominent South African Jews who emigrated
to Israel and took citizenship in the new nation was Abba
Eban, the distinguished Israeli diplomat.

The pro-Israel policy of the Nationalists had two closely
interrelated mainsprings, one ideological, the other geopolitical. Afrikaners considered themselves, like the ancient
Children of Israel, People of the Book, imbued with a
divine mission to build a religious civilization in the wilderness. Thus, *Die Burger*, the leading Nationalist newspaper,
could comment in May 1948: "The small Jewish community in Palestine, barely more than 600,000 strong,

[3]Henry Katzew, *Apartheid and Survival*. Cape Town: Simondium Publishers, 1965, p. 12.
[4]*Ibid.*, p. 13.

wishes to carve for itself and for racial brethren without a homeland a place on the map against the opposition of hostile states with a population of 30,000,000–40,000,000. If this is folly, then it is folly on an heroic scale."

Dr. Malan became the first Commonwealth Prime Minister to visit Israel. On his return, he told a Cape Town audience: "The greatness of a nation does not, after all, consist in the vastness of its wealth, but in the extent and greatness of its inward qualities of spirit and soul." He predicted that Israel would again have a message for the world.[5]

The geopolitical reason for South African support of Israel was the conviction that the Jewish state constituted a rampart, protecting Africa from the destructive and aggressive forces of Communism and Black nationalism. As Dr. Malan put the matter:

We have an interest in the defense of the Middle East, because that is the door through which the enemy will enter Africa. . . . Our interest is this, that Egypt and the Middle East is the gateway to Africa from the North. We have obligations in regard to the northern territories of Africa, because what happens higher up in Africa must necessarily affect us. Therefore, we have commitments toward the whole of Africa and toward the Middle East.

On April 24, 1952, Malan informed the House of Assembly that South Africa would cooperate with NATO in setting up the projected Middle East Command "to stop the enemy from coming through the Middle East and from invading Africa through Egypt in the event of war. We have undertaken to provide a division, apart from anything else which we may do at such a time. But this divi-

[5]Ibid., p. 13.

sion will not be sent there in time of peace. It will only be made available if war breaks out." While the Middle East Command never materialized, South Africa's interest in a rampart against Communist advance beyond Suez remained unchanged.

This preoccupation with the Communist threat to South Africa's existence was not confined to the Nationalist Party. Thus, when the Soviets destroyed Czechoslovakian democracy in February 1948, Jan Christian Smuts observed: "South Africa is not out of danger. . . . If the dam breaks, I see no point where the danger can be stopped. . . . Why declare war if the goal can be reached without it by means of infiltration? I believe the whole world will go down without war."[6]

Outlawing the Communist Party

The Communist Party had been accused of high treason in the *Botha Report* and the Nationalist Party was committed to take drastic steps against it. In 1949, the Government attempted to deprive such Red leaders as Solly Sachs, Sam Kahn and Dr. Yusef Dadoo, the Indian Communist leader, of their passports, but the courts generally ruled in favor of the plaintiffs. In April 1950, the Communist Party and the African National Congress announced their intention of holding "freedom day" demonstrations of non-Whites throughout the country. Fearing violence, the Government outlawed these meetings, but the Communists defied the order. Widespread demonstrations and riots occurred on April 26 on the Rand in which 18 people were killed.

The following month the Government introduced a bill

[6]J. C. Smuts, *op. cit.*, p. 414.

outlawing the Communist Party. The law defined Communism in very broad terms and included "any doctrine or scheme . . . which aims at bringing about any political, industrial or social change within the Union by the promotion of disturbance or disorder, by unlawful acts or omissions or by the threat of such acts or omissions. . . ." Conviction under this loosely drawn statute could result in a maximum penalty of ten years imprisonment.

Far more significant were the administrative weapons that the law established against Communist organization and propaganda. A liquidator was appointed to supervise the dissolution of Communist organizations and to compile a list of Communists, former Communists and Communist supporters. Unless they successfully rebutted the charge of Communist activity, they were forbidden to be members of Parliament, the Provincial Councils or other public bodies. Organizations serving the purposes of Communism were to be liquidated; broad powers were vested in the Government to suppress periodicals deemed Communist, and "named Communists" could be banned from attending trade union, political and other gatherings and could be barred from specific areas.

Although sharply criticized by the Johannesburg Bar as "a complete negation of the liberty of the subject as guaranteed by the rule of law," this measure faced little effective opposition in Parliament. The United Party, under its new leader, Jacobus Gideon Nel Strauss, opposed those provisions of the law that bypassed the courts, but proposed that judicial conviction of Communism be considered treason and punished under certain circumstances by death.

Since mere membership in the Communist Party was a prison offense, the Central Committee voted formally to dissolve over the opposition of Andrews and a few other diehards. This did not prevent the liquidator, Judge J. de Villiers Louw, from compiling lists of former activists and barring them from political activity. Among the first to be so named was Solly Sachs, the Garment Workers' Union leader. When Sachs defied the law by addressing a protest meeting, he was given a suspended prison sentence, which was sustained by the appellate court. Unable to carry on his organizational activity, Sachs departed for England.

The first Communist publication to be suppressed under the law was *The Guardian*, edited by Brian Bunting. Bunting simply changed the name of the publication after each suppression and thus it re-emerged briefly as *The Clarion, People's World, Advance* and *New Age*. The authorities eventually tired of this game and the appearance of the Red periodical under the name of *The Spark* was prevented by an administrative decision that Bunting and his associates were not to engage in editing or publishing any journal on pain of imprisonment[7]

Brian Bunting also accepted nomination for the House of Assembly, campaigned, was elected by a substantial majority of his non-White constituents, and then was ousted under the Suppression of Communism Act. Other Communists, among them Ray Alexander, also campaigned for elective offices they were not legally entitled to hold as a means of agitation and propaganda.

The African National Congress

The illegalization of the Party and the creation of an effective arsenal of weapons against it made it necessary

---

[7]Roux, *Time Longer Than Rope*, p. 382.

for the Communists to work through broad mass organizations. The opportunity to do this resulted from international disapproval of the Nationalist regime, its giant steps toward Apartheid and its resort to punitive measures against Communism, which aroused considerable opposition among South African liberals and intellectuals. Such opposition movements as the Torch Commandos, while attacked by Government officials as Communist-inspired, were in fact independent. In its efforts to build a mass opposition movement that the Government could not easily proscribe under the Suppression of Communism Act, the Party concentrated on the African National Congress.

Founded in 1912, the African National Congress had been an organization of Negro lawyers and political leaders that sought to appeal to the dominant White minority "in rational and constitutional terms" for an abatement of race discrimination and a share in government.[8] During World War II, younger leaders urged a more militant approach and Communist influence in the organization became substantial, if not controlling. In 1949, the Congress adopted the program of a tightly knit group of radicals who called themselves the Youth League. Of the able leaders of this latter group, Anton Lembede and R. M. Sobukwe were advocates of Black Power and the exclusion of Whites from participation. Walter Sisulu and Nelson Mandela were future leaders of the outlawed Communist Party who would be deeply implicated in its plans for sabotage and insurrectionary action.

There is a difference of opinion as to whether the African National Congress fell under Communist domination

[8]Rupert Emerson, *From Empire to Nation.* Cambridge: Harvard University Press, 1960, p. 243.

during World War II, in 1949 or shortly thereafter.[9] The precise date is not a matter of much importance. The 1949 Program of Action certainly was in conformity with Communist strategy and tactics. Its central theme was: ". . . freedom from White domination and the attainment of political independence. This implies the rejection of the conception of segregation, apartheid, trusteeship, or White leadership, which are all, in one way or another, motivated by the idea of White domination or the domination of White over Black."[10] The Congress proposed to make this goal a reality by disciplined passive resistance to racially discriminatory laws, on the one hand, and by the withdrawal of Bantu labor causing economic hardship to the nation, on the other.

A major difficulty faced by the African National Congress was the decapitation of its handful of competent leaders under the Suppression of Communism Act. Albert John Luthuli, the Zulu tribal chief who was to be awarded the Nobel Peace Prize in 1961 as a political gesture of opposition to South Africa, was banned from Congress activity in 1952 and again in 1954 and 1959. While Luthuli was not a Communist, he cooperated with Communists.[11] Walter Sisulu, the Secretary General of the Congress, a Xhosa of considerable native ability whose formal education had ceased at the fourth grade, was banned

[9]For varying views, see Edwin S. Munger, *Communist Activity in South Africa*. New York: American Universities Field Staff, ESM–8–'58, p. 21; Roux, *Time Longer Than Rope*, p. 403; Gerard Ludi and Blaar Grobbelaar, *The Amazing Mr. Fischer*. Cape Town: Nasionale Boekhandel, 1966, pp. 9–10.
[10]Edward Feit, *South Africa: The Dynamics of the African National Congress*. London: Institute of Race Relations, Oxford University Press, 1962, pp. 2–3.
[11]Albert Luthuli, *Let My People Go*. London: Collins, Fontana Books, 1962. "There are Communists in the South African resistance, and I cooperate with them." P. 137.

in 1952 and again in 1955. Oliver Tambo, another Negro Communist leader, replaced Sisulu as Secretary General and was banned in 1954 and 1959. The banned persons were permitted usually to participate in executive meetings and to address small gatherings, but they could not take part in mass meetings or demonstrations.

The Congress had very slender financial resources, few paid organizers and excessively large branches, some with a fluctuating membership of over 5,000. "Indiscipline was endemic," Feit reported.[12] Like other Communist-controlled organizations, the Congress engaged in factional struggles, spent a large part of its time and energy attacking the large African newspapers, in particular the largest, *The Bantu World*, alienated the wealthier non-Whites with its intolerance of dissent and supported only Communist periodicals such as the *New Age* and *Fighting Talk*.

The first major operation of the African National Congress, the Defiance Campaign, was planned jointly with the Communist-run Indian Congress and launched in February 1952. A call was issued for 10,000 volunteers openly to violate six laws that the Congress found obnoxious and to court arrest and imprisonment. The theory was that the prisons would become overcrowded; the police and judicial machinery would break down, and the Government would be compelled to consent to the nullification of its laws by mob action. The objectionable laws were characterized by the Defiance Campaign leaders as imposing racial segregation, but this was inexact. One was the Suppression of Communism Act and another was the compulsory culling of cattle on Bantu tribal lands, a measure essential to even the most rudimentary progress in Native animal husbandry.

[12]Feit, *op. cit.*, p. 20.

Some 8,000 persons, led by Patrick Duncan, son of a former Governor General of South Africa, and Manilal Gandhi, second son of the Mahatma, broke the laws by entering African locations without permission, by invading racially reserved railroad station waiting rooms and by similar actions. The initial result was substantially according to plan. The courts were crowded with hordes of offenders of comparatively minor laws. After the first confusion, however, the South African authorities reacted by arresting only known and suspected Communists. The campaign soon began to falter and by November, seven months after it had been launched, "had practically petered out."[13]

On international terrain, skillful Communist-inspired propaganda depicted the operation as a brilliant success. Its supposedly peaceful character was emphasized and the African National Congress gained world prestige as an organization able to follow in the footsteps of Gandhi. In fact, the Defiance Campaign had inflamed and unleashed primitive mobs. Violent riots had swept Johannesburg, East London, Kimberley and Port Elizabeth, but were put down by the police. In East London, mobs, incited by Communist agitators, indulged in rioting and arson. Dr. E. Quinn, a White nun who had attended to the Native sick in East London townships for many years, was dragged from her car and beaten and hacked to death. After they had set fire to her car, the rioters cut her body into small pieces and devoured it on the spot. When the police arrived on the scene, they shot and killed a number of the Native culprits without further ceremony.[14]

In 1953, a coordinating committee of the Communist

[13]Feit, *op. cit.*, p. 28.
[14]Chris Vermaak, *The Red Trap: Communism and Violence in South Africa.* Johannesburg: APB Publishers, 1966, p. 39.

rump trade union federation and the Red political organizations of Whites, Indians and Coloured, together with the African National Congress, was set up to plan a "Congress of the People" to draw up "a Freedom Charter for all peoples and all groups in South Africa. . . ."[15] Of the participating organizations, the most important was the Congress of Democrats, a White organization of from 350 to 500 members that had been set up as a Red cover organization when the Communist Party was illegalized.

What the C.O.D. lacked in popular support, it made up for in brains. It easily dominated the coordinating committee. According to the testimony of Dr. Peter Tsele, a prominent Native supporter of the multiracial policies of the Liberal Party in the 1950's and the enemy of any "totalitarian regime, be it white, black or red . . . ," bribery was one of the main means of control. He accused the Congress of Democrats of buying off the leadership of the African National Congress by "providing food and employment" and of libelling those who resisted its control by publishing false and defamatory charges against them in its press. Dr. Tsele also charged that the C.O.D. drafted the resolutions for African National Congress conventions six months in advance and, when necessary, ensured that they were passed by hiring unemployed Negroes to gatecrash the conventions as delegates.[16] The influential Bantu newspaper, *The World*, observed on May 28, 1958, that the "worst moment" of the African National Congress was "when it became an asylum of ex-Communists after the Government suppressed Communism in this country and drove it underground and made the Africans its prey."

Some 3,000 people showed up at the Congress of the

---

[15]Congress of Democrats, South African Indian Congress, South African Coloured People's Organization and the South African Congress of Trade Unions.

[16]Munger, *op. cit.*, pp. 21–23.

People which met at Kliptown on May 25–26, 1955. At the Congress, Luthuli called for 50,000 Freedom Volunteers to campaign for its program. Only a tenth of that number was recruited.

The Freedom Charter, which was approved at Kliptown, was a characteristically Communist *mélange* of Jeffersonian ideals, which served as window dressing, and of Socialist and totalitarian proposals. Asserting that "our people have been robbed of their birthright to land, liberty and peace by a government founded on injustice and inequality," the Charter demanded that all adults be given the vote regardless of race (or, for that matter, education or intelligence), that "the preaching and practice of national, race or color discrimination and contempt shall be a punishable crime," that the mineral wealth of the nation, banking and "monopoly industry" be nationalized, that rents and prices be lowered, and that "unused housing space shall be made available to the people." Moses Kotane, the General Secretary of the now disbanded Communist Party, saw the Charter as the initial step toward a "people's republic."[17]

The Freedom Charter, like the previous Defiance Campaign, had more impact on world liberal public opinion than it had within South Africa. With 28,000 members, according to the South African Government, and 100,000, according to Nelson Mandela, one of the Bantu Communists who had served as its Secretary General, the Congress never represented as many as 2 per cent of the Negro population. Since most of its members paid no dues and engaged in only sporadic activity in its behalf, membership was a somewhat nebulous concept. By contrast,

[17]Moses Kotane, *South Africa's Way Forward*. Cape Town, p. 8. Quoted by Feit, *op. cit.*, p. 15.

the Communists controlled about a third of the registered trade unions at the time the Party was illegalized,[18] completely dominated the strongest political force in the Indian community and had strong support, though very poor organization, among the Cape Coloured.[19]

Among the more significant open mass operations of the African National Congress were the Western Areas Campaign and the Bantu Education Campaign. The Western Areas were three townships—Sophiatown, Martindale and Newclare—in the outlying districts of Johannesburg. The city decided to raze these Black slums and resettle the displaced Bantu in new housing developments at Meadowlands and Diekploof.

The motives of the town authorities were mixed. As part of the general national policy of residential and territorial Apartheid, they wanted to eliminate all non-White enclaves within White areas. They were also concerned with the eradication of festering slums in which some 57,800 Blacks lived in 1,885 stands, "each stand being fifty feet by a hundred feet."[20] In addition to congestion, the Western Area townships were foci of disease and organized vice, in which the Negro population was terrorized by Bantu extortioners, robbers and murderers called *tsotsis*.[21] The *tsotsis*

[18]Since most of the Communist unions were small, this did not mean that the Reds controlled a third of the union membership and it emphatically did not mean that anything like a third of the organized workers were either Communists or Communist sympathizers.

[19]Munger, *op. cit.*, pp. 11–13.

[20]Feit, *op. cit.*, p. 37.

[21]*Tsotsi* means "something small" in Sesotho and denotes the stovepipe-bottom trousers that originally served to distinguish this criminal element. The *tsotsi* was characterized by J. C. de Ridder (*The Personality of the Urban African in South Africa: A Thematic Apperception Test Study,* London: Routledge & Kegan Paul, 1961, p. 6) as "an almost completely detribalized, often illegitimate, usually teenage criminal delinquent, who neither understands nor respects the tribal customs and culture of his forefathers. . . ."

modelled themselves on Chicago gangs during Prohibition as depicted in old movies.[22] They were in the habit of carving their gang marks inside the thighs of the prostitutes who hustled for them and of paralyzing those who resisted their demands by driving sharpened bicycle spokes into their spines. As a result in part of *tsotsi* activity, preoccupation with aggression and violence, generally of an intraracial sort, was and still is a predominant element in Bantu character structure.[23]

The Communists and the African National Congress agitated among the Bantu of the Western Areas to persuade them to refuse to leave their slums for the new housing developments. "The police managed to steal only 100 families; fifty were rescued by our gallant volunteers," the African National Congress Youth League reported.[24] The "rescued" families were neither able to return to their hovels, as the slums were being bulldozed out of existence, nor were they allowed to move to Meadowlands. For a while, the African National Congress activists put them up in shacks, but in a brief period of time tired of them and abandoned them to fend for themselves. When the Bantus received favorable reports from the migrants to Meadowlands and Diekploof, distrust of the African National Congress spread.

In December 1954, the Congress launched another and equally cynical mass campaign. To resist increasing race segregation in education, Negro parents were urged to

[22]"African *tsotsis* live in a kind of fantasy–world of American gangster films, for the *tsotsi* is a cinema addict and models his life and deeds on the actions of characters portrayed on the screen. Many *tsotsis* believe that the films are real in that they depict conditions in other countries." Laura Longmore, *The Dispossessed*. London: Corgi Books, 1966, p. 249.
[23]de Ridder, *op. cit.*, p. 154.
[24]*The Executive Report to the 12th Conference of the A.N.C. Youth League, 29th May 1955*. Unpublished. Quoted in Feit, *op. cit.*, p. 46.

boycott the public schools. The Congress leaders made no plans to continue the education of the children participating in the boycott until parental discontent induced them to promise a grandiose system of volunteer schools staffed by 1,000 teachers. The truant children were herded into halls and disused movie theatres without leadership or educational plan. "The children were unruly and unmanageable and the leaders were nonchalant," a Bantu reporter for the African tabloid, *Drum*, reported after visiting one of these "volunteer schools."[25] The teachers left the Congress schools because they were not paid and most of the children drifted away. Since the public schools for Bantu were already overcrowded, many of the children who took part in the boycott were unable to find places in them and abandoned schooling for the life of the streets.

Communist Party and Treason Trial

At the time of its suppression in 1950, the Communist Party of South Africa had a membership of approximately 2,500, of whom 1,200 were Bantu, 900 Whites, 250 Indians and 150 Coloured. Moses Kotane, the capable Negro General Secretary of the Party, travelled across South Africa, during the time when the Suppression of Communism Bill was being debated, closing Party cells, destroying or hiding compromising documents and issuing instructions to Party members to infiltrate mass organizations and work through them.[26] The Cape Town membership, including Sam Kahn, the former Congressman, opposed setting up an illegal Party, but was overruled. Under such highly intelligent Communist leaders as Joe Slovo and his

[25]*Drum*, November 1955, pp. 19–20.
[26]Munger, *op. cit.*, p. 36.

wife, Ruth First, the Johannesburg Party made an effective adjustment to the new conditions. In a comparatively brief period of time, a highly efficient, well disciplined illegal organization replaced the banned Party.

The liquidator of the Communist Party had named about 600 persons under the Suppression of Communism Act by 1958. Evidence of an individual's Party membership would be heard *in camera* and would often consist of depositions by informers, truants and undercover police agents. There were a number of cases in which the chief magistrate entrusted with liquidation refused to name persons under the Act because he judged the Government's evidence to be inadequate.

The 600-odd named persons probably provide a fairly good cross section of the leadership cadres and militants of the Party during the early 1950's. Of the 235 Europeans, 74 were women and over a third were born abroad, primarily in Eastern Europe and Britain. Johannesburg had a bit over half the White membership and Cape Town more than a quarter of them. Of the 256 Africans, about half lived in Johannesburg, Pretoria and adjacent towns. In terms of tribal affiliation, there were 85 Basuto, 54 Xhosa and 19 Zulu. Large tribal groups had remained untouched by Communist organization. There were also 46 Asians and 67 Cape Coloured among the persons named.[27]

On September 17, 1955, the Special Branch of the South African National Police concerned with the suppression of Communism raided the homes and offices of some 400 individuals and organizations suspected of treasonable activity and seized an enormous harvest of documents, pamphlets, books and other literature. After studying this mate-

[27]*Ibid.*, pp. 37–38.

rial for over a year, the Government arrested 156 people, most of whom had been prominent either in the Communist Party or in the African National Congress or both, and brought them to Johannesburg to stand trial for treason.

The Treason Trial aroused international attention and generated the spate of liberal protests to be expected. The persons accused were in fact a bizarre political amalgam. Most of the known leaders of the Communist Party were among the defendants, but the latter also included Chief Albert Luthuli, the Congress leader who was later to win the Nobel Peace Prize; Len Lee-Warden, Native representative for the Western Cape; Professor Z. K. Matthews, the acting head of Fort Hare College (a Bantu institution); and one European Methodist and two Bantu African clergymen.[28]

The Government based its case on attempted proof of the allegation that the African National Congress, and its Freedom Charter in particular, were revolutionary attempts to bring about a political, social and economic change in South Africa by force and violence. Expert testimony was introduced, notably that of Professor Andrew Murray of the University of Cape Town, to the effect that the verbiage of seized African National Congress documents was similar to that of Lenin and Stalin and of avowed Communist publications. The defense lawyers, including Queen's Counsellor Braam Fischer, who was known to most South Africans as one of their ablest legal minds and was unknown to them in his clandestine role as architect of the illegal Communist Party apparatus, found it easy to make Professor Murray look foolish. At one point,

[28]Carter, *op. cit.*, p. 378.

the Professor, under cross-examination, identified sentences as Communist in phraseology that were then shown to be from his own writings.

The Government unexpectedly dropped its case against 61 of the 91 defendants, but showed poor judgment in its choice of hard-core elements for prosecution. Seven former card-carrying members of the banned Communist Party were released, but Dr. Z. K. Matthews, who had deliberately remained aloof from the Communist defendants, was made to stand trial. As the trial droned on year after year, it gave leaders of South African Communism the world-wide publicity they needed and, moreover, enabled them to appear to be victims of fascist injustice. The trial "played into Communist hands to the extent that it has given a sense of common unity to those who find them-selves under attack by the Government."[29] Moreover, like most efforts to base a treason or sedition trial primarily on interpretation of political writings, it ended in the same sort of fiasco that the United States Government encoun-tered when it failed to convict 30 alleged Nazi seditionists during World War II.[30] In March 1961, Mr. Justice Rumpff passed judgment. He found that only a small per-centage of the African National Congress documents urged violence, that, while the Congress had "a strong left-wing tendency," the Government had not proved that it was

[29]Munger, *op. cit.*, pp. 41–42.

[30]Nathaniel Weyl, *Treason*. Washington: Public Affairs Press, 1950, p. 340. Substantially what I wrote about that trial could be repeated con-cerning the South African one: "The alleged seditionists should certainly have been tried and some might well have been convicted—but not as the Department of Justice handled the case. The spectacular mass political trial in Washington gave off a faint scent of Nazi and Communist pro-cedure. The accused were not brought to the bar to answer for the con-crete and tangible things they had actually done. They were instead accused of forming part of a worldwide Nazi conspiracy. The evidence to substantiate this grandiose charge was not available to the Government at the time the indictment was laid."

Communist-controlled and that the prosecution had also failed to prove that the Congress intended to achieve the changes it desired "by violent means."

Meanwhile, a major rift had appeared in the radical Negro movement of South Africa. In 1958, Black Power advocates made a determined, but unsuccessful, effort to wrest control of the African National Congress from the Communist element that ran it. In the following year, the dissidents held a conference at Orlando with 300 delegates and launched a new movement, the Pan Africanist Congress.[31] Its leader was Robert Sobukwe, a lecturer in Bantu languages at the University of Witwatersrand. He demanded that membership in the new movement be confined to Africans, a proviso that was later modified to admit a few Whites, notably Patrick Duncan, at the insistence of European revolutionaries who were financing the organization. Sobukwe asserted that the only way to reach the Bantu masses was by direct action of a revolutionary sort against the racial laws. He proposed a nationwide movement to disobey the pass laws under the slogan "No bail, no defense, no fine" and predicted that the P.A.C. civil disobedience movement would signal the beginning of the end of White rule in South Africa.

The day chosen was March 21, 1960. Far from being nationwide, the civil disobedience movement was confined to Sharpeville and Langa, virtually the only places where the Pan Africanist Congress had a mass following. Ten thousand Negroes surrounded the Sharpeville police station, demanded to be arrested and hurled rocks at the police.[32]

Possibly nervous because of an incident that had oc-

[31]Also called the Pan African Congress.
[32]Roux, *Time Longer Than Rope*, p. 406.

curred two months previously at Cato Mano, near Durban, in which a Negro mob had butchered four White and five African policemen, the police began to fire on the crowd. Volley after volley was discharged into their ranks before the responsible police officers ordered that the firing cease. When the smoke cleared, 67 Bantu were dead and 186 wounded. Two truckloads of corpses were taken to the morgue.

There was a direct conflict of testimony before the one-man commission of inquiry, consisting of Mr. Justice P. J. Wessels, that investigated the affair, between those who asserted that the crowd had been peaceful and the police, who claimed that it had been about to attack them. Justice Wessels was unable to establish who gave the order to fire and he concluded that there had been no organized attempt to seize the police station. Sharpeville created worldwide indignation and further damaged South Africa's image. Regardless of the intentions of the mob, police violence had been disproportionate to the provocation.

The Sharpeville massacre gave the Pan Africanist Congress great prestige among the politically active Bantu. On March 31, it was able to mobilize 25,000 Natives in Cape Town to protest mass arrests of radicals. On April 8, both the African National Congress and the Pan Africanist Congress were banned under an Unlawful Organizations Act, which further tightened the noose around the remaining revolutionary mass organizations of South Africa.

❖ ❖ ❖ ❖ ❖

CHAPTER EIGHT

Ordeal by Terror in Angola

"Happiness lies only in that which excites and the only thing that excites is crime."

—DONATIEN ALPHONSE FRANÇOIS,
MARQUIS DE SADE

THE ELECTION OF JOHN F. KENNEDY TO THE AMERICAN Presidency in November 1960 was a tocsin of imminent danger for South Africa and the other White-ruled states south of the Zambesi. During the three years that Kennedy occupied the White House, the Communist offensive in Southern Africa would reach its greatest intensity, external pressure on the nations and dependencies of that region would rise toward a crescendo, and the White and Black inhabitants of Portugal's African possessions would undergo a fearful calvary.

While still a Senator, Kennedy had made it quite clear that he was prepared to support independence movements in the so-called underdeveloped areas of the world, even where their Communist affiliations were evident, against America's European allies. In 1957, Kennedy touched off anti-American demonstrations in France by publicly urging President Eisenhower to take steps to recognize the "independent personality of Algeria," a strange phrase since Algeria had never been a nation and did not exist as a unified territory prior to French rule. This venture into international politics drew the caustic comment from Secretary of State Dulles that, if Kennedy were really interested in crusading against colonialism, he might speak out against the institution in its Soviet form.[1]

Less than a week after Kennedy's inauguration as President, a motley group of Spanish, Portuguese, Venezuelan and Cuban Communists, anarchists and disgruntled politicians seized the Portuguese liner, *Santa Maria*, on the high seas during a routine cruise. Using the technique of Chinese river pirates, the invaders posed as passengers to get aboard, then overpowered the crew and murdered a young Portuguese officer.

This audacious operation was planned by the Iberian Revolutionary Directorate of Liberation (D.R.I.L.), with headquarters in Cuba. The chief leaders of this organization included Santiago Carrillo, General Secretary of the illegal Communist Party of Spain; "General" Alberto Bayo, the Communist veteran of the Spanish Civil War who had trained Fidel Castro's invasion force in Mexico in 1956;[2] and Antonio Nuñez Jiménez, a Cuban Communist of long standing who represented the Castro regime.[3] Some of the weapons and all of the forged passports and other docu-

---

[1]James MacGregor Burns, *John Kennedy*. New York: Harcourt, Brace & Company, 1959, pp. 195–96.
[2]His real rank was major.
[3]Henry Josti Russell, *Santa Maria Ahoy*. Lisbon: Edições Panorama, 1961, p. 139.

mentation for the pirates were supplied by the Cuban and Venezuelan Communist organizations.[4]

When the *Santa Maria* was seized, Humberto Delgado, a former Portuguese presidential candidate in self-imposed exile in Brazil, assumed responsibility for the piracy and informed the Rio de Janeiro Communist newspaper, *Ultima Hora*, that the aim of the operation was the total "liberation" of Spain and Portugal.[5] The operational leader of this extraordinary venture was a former Portuguese Army captain named Henrique Galvão, who had formerly been a propagandist for the Nazis and an invited guest of Adolf Hitler,[6] but who had apparently switched to the Communists after the Fuehrer's downfall. A thoroughly unstable individual who once boasted of having planted bombs in Madrid, Barcelona and other Spanish cities, Galvão appeared on the *Santa Maria* in a uniform of his own design that promoted him from captain to four-star general.[7]

When news of the act of piracy was flashed around the world, dozens of newspaper, magazine and radio reporters were flown to Portuguese Angola on the southwest coast of Africa because they had been informed that the *Santa Maria* proposed to land there and commence a revolution against Portuguese rule in Africa. If the original target was Angola, it was soon abandoned because Portuguese naval units were promptly deployed to intercept any attack on that colony.

The American reaction was interesting. Immediately after the seizure of the vessel on January 25, 1961, Lincoln White, the holdover State Department spokesman from the Eisenhower Administration, was asked whether Galvão

[4]*Ibid.*, p. 133.
[5]*Ibid.*, pp. 76–77.
[6]*Nation Belge*, February 26, 1961.
[7]Russell, *op. cit.*, pp. 27, 92.

and his men might seek political asylum. "That seems a little far-fetched," he replied. "If they are mutineers, they are mutineers, and no question of political asylum is involved." Simultaneously, the Department of Defense stressed that American Fleet units were seeking to intercept the *Santa Maria* in accordance with the international law of piracy.

As the Kennedy Administration began to take over control, the official attitude of the United States changed. On January 25, the *New York Times* editorialized against punitive action. "To endanger the lives of so many innocent men, women and children and to risk such a valuable property," it argued, "is neither funny nor excusable." The following day, the *New York Herald Tribune* speculated: "Possibly Henrique Galvão simply desired to dramatize opposition to (Portuguese President) Salazar." These opinions may well have been administration-inspired trial balloons. On January 27, a U.S. Navy spokesman indicated that the original purpose of putting down an act of piracy had been abandoned, stating: "To trail the ship and keep its position . . . We have no instructions to keep the *Santa Maria* from entering any port."[8]

The *Neue Züricher Zeitung*, one of the best newspapers on the European continent, noted that the great powers seemed to be abandoning their obligations under international law. After showing cogently why the seizure of the *Santa Maria* constituted a clear-cut case of piracy, it observed:

It is the duty of every and any country, by every means at their disposal, to detain the pirate ship, arrest the pirates and free the passengers and crew.

[8]Russell, *op. cit.*, p. 71.

The convention dealing with rights on the high seas, signed in Geneva on April 29th, 1958, constitutes an authoritative list of rules of international law as recognized today, and which all states may invoke, whether or not they subscribed to the convention. Portugal may, therefore, not only undertake the pursuit of the ship with her own warships but may also demand of other members of the community of nations that they too shall contribute in every way toward the arrest of the pirates.[9]

Despite the obligations of the United States under international law, the Kennedy Administration deployed naval units around the *Santa Maria* and arranged a deal by which the pirates disembarked in a Brazilian port where they were assured safety by the leftist government of that country. The cruise liner was returned to its Portuguese owners. Eleven days after the seizure, on February 5, Communists and other opposition elements attempted an uprising in the city of Luanda, Angola, but were easily crushed. As for Humberto Delgado, who had taken responsibility for the act of piracy, his corpse was discovered near the Portuguese-Spanish border on April 24, 1965, and was identified by the Spanish Ministry of Justice on May 8. There were indications that he had died a violent death, whether at the hands of the Portuguese police, at those of some of his former co-conspirators or at those of others remains unknown.

Massacre in Angola

Portugal became the favorite whipping boy of the Kennedy Administration. The reasons for this seemed somewhat obscure since Portugal's policies were more liberal on the race issue than those of the other European colonial

[9]January 11, 1961.

powers. As for Angola, an area of about half a million square miles of savannah climate, comparable in size to France, Germany, Spain and Portugal combined, its Portuguese settlers were primarily peasants, tradespeople, officials and soldiers who had come there, not to make their fortunes or do a brief stint at some governmental post, but to raise families and strike roots in Angolese soil. The Portuguese were not newcomers to the land, but had made their first landfall some years before Columbus discovered America.

In Angola, Mozambique and Portugal's other African possessions, there was and is a minimum of color prejudice. The distinguished Brazilian sociologist, Gilberto Freyre, attributed this attitude to the fact that Christian Portugal was for centuries exposed to and ruled by Moors whose level of civilization was in some respects superior to its own. Accordingly, the Portuguese, whether at home, in Brazil or in their overseas possessions, never acquired that association between dark skin-pigmentation and inferiority, which is such a prominent element in the heritage of northern Europeans.[10] In Angola, all public accommodations were open to both races; schools were racially integrated; Blacks and Whites worked side by side on the same jobs; there was no resentment of non-Whites bossing Whites; racial intermarriage was accepted socially and, in many instances, encouraged by governmental policy.

At the time of the uprising, the population of Angola consisted of about 5 million tribal Africans and 75,000 *assimilados* (assimilated people). The latter were those Whites and Blacks who satisfied the minimal property and educational qualifications for full Portuguese citizenship

[10]Gilberto Freyre, *Brazil, an Interpretation*. New York: Alfred A. Knopf, 1945, pp. 19–22.

and who opted for such citizenship. Since citizenship carried such obligations as paying taxes and bearing arms, not all eligible Africans desired it.[11] The fact that only a small minority of the total population enjoyed citizenship rights enabled some liberal critics of Portuguese policies to claim that assimilation was a sham and that the realities of the situation were rule by a small, largely White minority and a subordinate status for the mass of Africans. It was, of course, true that the tribal Africans, who appear even more primitive than the South African Bantu,[12] formed the lowest level of the social and economic pyramid, but this reflected their cultural condition and was not imposed upon them because of their race.

Whether the Portuguese policy of fostering integration and biological assimilation was wise or foolish, whether it is likely to produce a civilization of hybrid vigor or to result in genetic impoverishment are matters on which there is wide difference of opinion. What was indisputable was that Portugal was practicing racial integration with more consistency and determination than any other White power. Angola and Mozambique were not colonies, but integral parts of Portugal. The Portuguese objective was not the traditional British one of preserving tribal institutions while mitigating their cruelty and irrationality, but full citizenship for all.[13] Perhaps as a gesture to international liberal opinion, Portugal abandoned the concept of *assimilados* in the fall of 1961 and made all Angolans Portuguese citizens, while retaining modest educational and property qualifications for the franchise.

[11]Bernardo Teixeira, *The Fabric of Terror.* New York: Devin-Adair Company, 1965, p. 162.
[12]Personal observation when in Angola in 1965.
[13]By contrast, Mussolini once declared that he wanted to make his Ethiopian subjects "good Africans and not bad Europeans."

The Kennedy Administration chose to ignore Portugal's efforts to create a multiracial society in her African territories. Its anti-European and anti-White bias was demonstrated in Arthur M. Schlesinger's partisan history of the administration. Schlesinger characterized the Portuguese Government as "hopelessly anchored in its medieval certitudes" and added: "Of all the classical colonial countries, Portugal was by far the most impervious to the winds of change."[14] Whether or not President Kennedy shared these unhistoric judgments, his determination to undercut America's NATO ally and strip her of her African possessions soon became obvious. When Liberia put a resolution before the UN Security Council calling on Portugal to abandon colonialism, Ambassador to the United Nations Adlai E. Stevenson supported the proposal, adding the unctuous assertion that the United States did so as "a friend of Portugal." Even with American support, the Liberian proposal failed of passage, but the Communist-led Negro terrorists who coveted Angola now realized that they had at least the benevolent neutrality of the United States.

On the morning of March 15, 1961, bands of Angolese and Congolese Negroes made simultaneous and unprovoked attacks on the isolated settlements in the Uige district of northern Angola. In a letter to the London *Times*, dated July 4, 1961, the British geologist William I. Stanton, who was an eyewitness, pointed out that "the present emergency began with the premeditated slaughter by Africans of more than 800 Portuguese, including hundreds of women and children," who were "mutilated, disembowelled, hacked to pieces." He added: "The reaction to news of Black and White atrocities is a bitter comment on the

[14]Arthur M. Schlesinger, Jr., A *Thousand Days*. Boston: Houghton Mifflin Company, 1965, p. 511.

state of color prejudice in Britain. Press and radio raise their voices in fury when an African is bayoneted by a Portuguese soldier. But when Africans cut the hands and feet off a Portuguese child, pluck out her eyes, and stick her mother's head on a pole—no one says a word."

In his report to the United Nations, Portuguese Ambassador Vasco Garin gave some details of the atrocities committed:

A witness . . . heard the prolonged cries of agony of those being quartered because the terrorists, their victims still alive, plucked their eyes out, cut off their heads, tore pieces of flesh from their bodies, disembowelled them and committed other bestial acts. Some Whites, Mulattoes and Negroes were skinned alive. . . .

The women, regardless of their age, were dragged from their houses by the terrorists. Their children were snatched from them. The bodies of these innocent victims were then used to play ball with. All children's hands and feet were cut off. . . . Girls were raped. All women, regardless of their age, had their clothes ripped off prior to being raped several times by bands of savages. . . . These scenes occurred during the assault on the M'bridge plantation. The name of the survivor who told the tale and is still convalescent is Manuel Lourenço Neves Alves. The terrorists who assaulted that plantation were not known locally. The attack took place on March 15th.[15]

The leader of the invasion was a Bakongo Negro, who had been educated at a Baptist mission school and was married to a White woman of British origin. Known variously as Holden Roberto, Roberto Holden, José Gilmore, Ruy Ventura, Onofre, etc., he became a professional revo-

[15]These atrocities were not confined to the M'bridge plantation, but were the general rule. For grisly details and photographs, see Teixeira, *op. cit.* I am convinced of the accuracy of the Portuguese reports from having examined dozens of photographs of mutilated victims and having talked to survivors personally.

lutionary when he founded the Union of the Peoples of Angola (UPA) in 1954. A friend and disciple of such Communist and pro-Communist leaders as Sekou Touré, Kwame Nkrumah and Patrice Lumumba, Roberto was in contact with Soviet Ambassador Solod in Conakry in 1958 and with various other Russian and Chinese agents.

In August 1959, Holden Roberto visited the United States where he was given the red-carpet treatment by "the State Department, the Central Intelligence Agency, the AFL-CIO officials concerned with international affairs, and Mrs. Eleanor Roosevelt. These contacts bore fruit; henceforth Roberto and the UPA got both financial and political support from United States sources."[16]

Back in the Congo, Roberto acquired the powerful patronage of Patrice Lumumba, the pro–Russian Communist leader, and proceeded to set up training camps and to transform the UPA into a disciplined revolutionary organization. Recruits were obtained from the Bakongo tribesmen in northern Angola "by the traditional Communist tactic of sending leaders into African villages, killing and mutilating a number of men *pour encourager les autres,* and threatening the remainder of the men with like treatment if they did not join the terrorist advance. Wholesale use has been made of the influence of witch doctors, fetishism, and residuary cannibalism."[17]

Using these methods, Roberto recruited a force of about 5,000 Angolan and Congolese Natives, mostly Bakongos, armed them with rifles and machetes left behind by the Belgian constabulary and stimulated their courage with

[16]James Burnham in Teixeira, *op. cit.,* p. 168.
[17]Hugh Kay, "A Catholic View," in British Institute of Race Relations, *Angola: Views of a Revolt.* London: Oxford University Press, 1962. Quoted in Teixeira, *op. cit.,* p. 169.

drugs. The declared objective was to slaughter all Whites. Probably Roberto believed that he could spread such terror among the isolated farms and settlements of northern Angola that the White settlers would flee in panic and the Negro tribes hostile to the Bakongos would submit. After the apparent success of the first blow, the strength of the UPA armed bands rose to reach a maximum of about 25,000 men.

The ignorance and stupidity of the Africans facilitated recruitment. A Portuguese major told Teixeira that 26 of the latest batch of terrorists captured had been recruited by the promise of cabinet posts and ambassadorships to the United Nations even though two-thirds of them were illiterate. "Among them was a boy, only fifteen, who was persuaded by the UPA to murder his foster father, a White doctor, with the promise that he would receive the doctor's shining instruments and his diploma to practice medicine."[18]

The American Reaction

On March 16, the day after Holden Roberto's dope-crazed tribesmen had butchered thousands of White settlers and their Black workers in the ways already alluded to, Adlai E. Stevenson, President Kennedy's new Ambassador to the United Nations, announced a reversal of traditional American policy. Declaring that he had the President's specific "approval," Stevenson supported the Russian resolution for "immediate steps . . . to transfer all power to the peoples" of Africa "without any conditions or reservations. . . ." His justification for this decision that

[18]Teixeria, *op. cit.*, p. 27.

the Angola tribesmen were fit for self-government was the expected quotation from Thomas Jefferson's statement that "all men are created equal."[19]

The terrorist invasion of Angola was consistently represented by President Kennedy's spokesmen as a popular movement of the oppressed African people for their liberation. "Angola, Mozambique and Portuguese Guinea were all in conditions of incipient revolt," Schlesinger wrote in his pseudo-history, "and the new African states were determined to help them gain their freedom."[20] The facts of the matter, as Professor Schlesinger should have known given his access to State Department dispatches, were that the mass base of support of the UPA was confined virtually to the Bakongo tribe, which accounted for only one-tenth of Angola's Black population and which was cordially hated by the other tribes. The "incipient revolt" in Mozambique and Portuguese Guinea was largely imaginary. The notion that the purpose of the insurgent movement was to gain "freedom" was negated by the fact that Holden Roberto's force preached and practiced genocide and the further fact that the UPA was under Communist control.

The radicals, who consistently advocated an American policy in support of Black Africa, even where this involved alienation of European allies of the United States, were almost all newcomers to the Government who had been taken mostly from professorial chairs and placed by President Kennedy in positions of bureaucratic power. They included Arthur M. Schlesinger, Jr., Adlai E. Stevenson and Harlan Cleveland at the United Nations, Chester Bowles, Mennen Williams, Kennedy's choice to run Afri-

[19]As Stevenson undoubtedly knew, Jefferson did not believe that all men are born with equal ability, intelligence and moral character, but the exact contrary.
[20]Schlesinger, *op. cit.*, p. 562.

can affairs in the State Department, and Roger Hilsman.[21] To their credit, it should be said that most seasoned State Department and Pentagon officials opposed the new cloud-cuckoo-land policies as adverse to American interests and likely to further the advance of Communism.

President Kennedy's crusade to force Portugal to relinquish her African possessions encountered the stumbling block that the U.S. base in the Portuguese Azores, which the Joint Chiefs of Staff had recently declared essential to national security in the event of a new Berlin crisis,[22] was coming up for renewal. Kennedy went to Secretary of Defense Robert Strange McNamara and was informed by that official that political considerations should override national security exigencies in determining relations with Portugal.

Arthur Krock, the Washington correspondent of the *New York Times,* took sharp issue with the Kennedy-Stevenson policy toward Portuguese Africa despite the fact that his paper editorially supported the radicals. He wrote that Ambassador Stevenson's support of instant self-government for Angola Blacks was "totally irresponsible and an incitement to more violence," adding that no responsible American could urge turning over total power to people who had just committed the atrocities incident to the March 15 invasion. Krock warned that the United States should not try to compete with the Soviet Union in a "popularity contest." A power bent on destroying the existing social order, he thought, can always urge more extreme measures than one with a national interest in preserving that order.

Stevenson's support of the U.N. resolution that con-

[21]Roger Hilsman, *To Move a Nation.* Garden City: Doubleday & Company, 1967, pp. 376–77.
[22]Schlesinger, *op. cit.,* p. 562.

demned Portugal for "severely repressive measures" in Angola seemed to Krock simply immoral and "a form of lynch
law." He observed that the United States had joined in this
condemnation despite the fact that the commission appointed by the United Nations to investigate conditions in
Angola had not issued its report. Moreover, Adlai Stevenson had committed the United States to following the new
Afro-Asian states in refusing to condemn "the murderous
attacks of the Angolese against Portuguese settlers." When
the Kennedy Administration treated America's Portuguese
ally in this shabby fashion, Krock added, it was undermin-
ing NATO and impairing the security of Western Europe.

Turning of the Tide

Portugal flew in troops from the peninsula to stem the
invasion and restore order. When the smoke had cleared,
it appeared that the terrorists had slaughtered about 1,500
Whites and 20,000 Blacks. Aided by armed White settlers
and Negroes loyal to the regime, the Portuguese armed
forces began to mop up the guerrilla bands, driving the
main insurgent force across the 1,300-mile border between
Angola and the Congo. Those Negroes who had been
forced to join the terrorists, generally because their tribal
chiefs were ordered to choose between furnishing a quota
of conscripts or being killed, were pardoned.

By mid-1962, Portugal claimed officially that order had
been restored in all but 2 per cent of Angolan territory.
The insurgent forces were further weakened by a factional
struggle between the different revolutionary parties. The
murder of Patrice Lumumba shortly after Kennedy's inauguration further weakened the position of Holden Roberto.

The shock of the rebellion made Portugal act swiftly to

modernize her African possessions and create conditions under which a repetition of the March 15 massacre would be impossible. Civil engineering projects, some of them military, but also including new hospitals, schools and housing developments, were rushed toward completion. The discovery of highly promising oil reserves in Angola and of new deposits of high-grade iron ore triggered a swift economic development that continued throughout the 1960's.

In 1965, Portugal liberalized the conditions governing the influx of foreign capital into her African territories. Intensified South African investment in Mozambique and heavy capital flow into Angola, mainly of West German origin, resulted. In both Angola and Mozambique, the Portuguese Government sponsored large new agricultural settlements of fertile, but heretofore untilled, land. In some instances, these colonies were organized on the basis of a checkerboard pattern of White and Black agricultural settlement.

A considerable immigration of Portuguese settlers, a growth of population in Angola's cities and a large-scale program of public investment in hydroelectric power and irrigation works in Mozambique further contributed to the reinforcement of Portugal's African footholds. "If five years ago, Portugal's position in Africa seemed precarious," a South African observer wrote in 1966, "there is today little doubt as to the permanency of the Portuguese presence in the foreseeable future."[23]

In December 1968, Frank Judd, a Labour Member of Parliament, asked British Secretary of Defense Dennis Healey for assurance that "arms supplied for the defense of

[23]"Angola and Mozambique," *Bulletin of the Africa Instituut*, Pretoria, Vol. IV, No. 3, (March 1966), p. 54.

freedom and democracy will never be used for the suppression of freedom fighters in Portuguese territories of Africa or elsewhere." Mr. Healey gave that assurance. Thereupon, Mr. John Bigg-Davison, a Conservative M.P., asked: "Since Her Majesty's Government rely on the security of such territories (as Angola and Mozambique) for communications round the Cape, is not this attitude a lot of humbug?" Mr. Healey refused to agree that he or his opinions were humbug and spoke of "the natural desire of African peoples for independence."

The terrorists also enjoyed a certain amount of support from American missionaries. In an article in *The Scotsman* of Edinburgh, Major McKeon, a retired British Army officer who was on active duty against the Mau Mau in Kenya and who had recently returned from Angola, commented: "There is evidence in Angola of American missions, particularly Baptist, conducting subversive activities against the (Portuguese) administration. . . ." He added that there had been similar "indignation in Kenya at what is considered as American interference in the colony, and this was particularly evident during the Mau Mau emergency. I discussed this matter generally with a number of foreign nationals and several consuls; the general consensus of opinion was that the American missionaries had overstepped the mark by entering the political field and deserved the consequences that followed."[24] It will be recalled that Holden Roberto, the man responsible for the grisly massacre in Angola, was a product of Baptist mission schooling.

Poor in material resources, but not in spirit, Portugal continued to shoulder the burden of the defense of her African possessions. If necessary, it seemed clear that Rhodesia

[24]November 9, 1961.

and South Africa would assume whatever part of the onus was necessary to guard the Zambesi River, natural frontier of civilization in Africa south of the Sahara. The defeat of the Democratic Administration in the United States in 1968 and the growing disgust of the British public with their Labour Government seemed auguries of a less fanatically hostile policy toward White rule on the African continent.

❖ ❖ ❖ ❖ ❖

CHAPTER NINE

The Insurrectionaries of Rivonia

"These documents clearly revealed that the accused deliberately and maliciously plotted and engineered the commission of acts of violence and destruction throughout the country. . . . The planned purpose thereof was to bring about in the Republic of South Africa chaos, disorder and turmoil which would be aggravated, according to their plans, by the operation of thousands of trained guerrilla warfare units deployed throughout the country at various vantage points. These would be joined in the various areas by local inhabitants as well as by selected men posted to such areas. The combined operations were planned to lead to confusion, violent insurrection and rebellion followed at the appropriate juncture by an armed invasion of the country by military units of foreign powers. In the midst of the resulting chaos, disorder and turmoil, it was planned by the accused to set up a provisional revolutionary government. . . . The accused admitted the authenticity of all these documents, and also that their policy included the eventual overthrow of the Government of South Africa by violence. It is because of this that I submitted to the Court that this was a case of high treason *par excellence*, and it was on those facts found proved which constituted the crime, no matter by what name the crime may be called, that the accused were duly found guilty."

—Dr. Percy Yutar, *prosecuting attorney at the Rivonia trial*

By the early 1960's, the South African Communist Party was efficiently organized on an illegal basis. At the bottom were racially segregated cells, the purpose of the segregation being to avoid the police attention which racially mixed gatherings might invite. One man served as courier between each cell and the next higher echelon, the Area Committee, and he was the only person who knew the membership and headquarters of both groups. Contact between Area and District Committees was maintained in the same fashion. The Center, which directed the activities of the entire Communist movement in South Africa, was also linked to each District Committee by one and only one courier. Accordingly, mass arrests at any echelon would not normally jeopardize the security of the Communist functionaries at higher echelons.

The Communist Party membership was divided into four categories. The first three of these comprised people who might easily fall under police surveillance: listed Communists, both in and out of jail, and police suspects who were not known to be Communists. The fourth category comprised individuals whose revolutionary activities were entirely unknown to the police. This group met in cells of its own as an essential security measure.[1]

The Party decided on a course of violence in the spring or summer of 1961, and in the middle of that year Joe Slovo, the Johannesburg attorney who had played such a prominent part in building an illegal Communist organization, informed the Johannesburg District Committee that

[1]Ludi and Grobbelaar, *op. cit.*, pp. 30–31. This book is a valuable source on the organization and operations of the illegal Communist Party of South Africa during the early 1960's Its senior author, Gerard Ludi, was an underground Communist while serving as Secret Agent Q-018 of the Security Branch of the South African police.

the Center had decided to concentrate on sabotage.[2] At approximately the same time, Nelson Mandela, one of the two most able Bantu Communists in South Africa, met with other leaders of the African National Congress and formed a new illegal organization, *Umkhonto We Sizwe*, meaning "the Spear of the Nation."[3] *Umkhonto* was set up as a combat organization to organize sabotage throughout South Africa and to move later from sabotage to insurrectionary forms of struggle.

The sabotage campaign was launched on Dingaan's Day, December 16, 1961, with bomb outrages against electrical installations and Federal Government and municipal offices, in which one person was killed.[4] In the wake of the sabotage campaign, scare leaflets were placed in the mail boxes of White people under the signature of the African National Congress.

"LISTEN, WHITE MAN!" one of them began.

Five Whites were murdered in the Transkei, another hacked to death at Langa. . . . Sabotage erupts every other week throughout the country, now here, now there. The Whites are turning vicious and panicky. . . . At this rate, within a year or two South Africa will be embroiled in the second, bloodier, more furious, Algerian war.

SABOTAGE AND MURDER MULTIPLIED LAST YEAR.

SABOTAGE AND MURDER WILL NOT CEASE.

You now face an indefinitely long future of terror, uncertainty and steadily eroding power. You will keep a gun at your side, not knowing whom to trust. Perhaps the street-cleaner is a saboteur, perhaps the man who makes your tea at the office

---

[2]*Ibid.*, p. 36.
[3]Mary Benson, *The Struggle for a Birthright*. London: Penguin African Series, 1966, p. 237. A pro–Communist source, this volume is more accurate in its factual account than judicious in its interpretations.
[4]*Ibid.*, p. 237.

has a gun. . . . You will never be safe and you will never be sure. YOU WILL HAVE LAUNCHED A WAR YOU CANNOT WIN.[5]

The decision of the Communist Party to turn toward violence as its main strategy of struggle and to intensify this struggle, stage by stage, from nationwide sabotage to armed insurrection and civil war was based on several considerations. Of these, probably the most important was that the repressive legislation of the Nationalists had virtually stifled the mass-action campaigns of prior years. A second, and perhaps equally important, factor was the inauguration of President Kennedy in the United States and the shift in American policy toward all-out support of the "instant freedom" demands of the Black African states. Communist analyses of strategy during the Kennedy-Johnson era (and particularly during the period of President Kennedy's incumbency) stressed the international support which South African Communist movements could expect, not only from the Soviet and Afro-Asian blocs, but from the United States as well. The Labour Party leaders, and particularly such leftwingers as Barbara Castle, had been for many years politically associated with and sympathetic to such front organizations of South African Communism as the African National Congress.

Poqo's Murder Campaigns

Poqo, meaning "pure," the terrorist branch of the Pan African Congress, was probably launched as early as the winter of 1961. Based on Mau Mau experience in Kenya, Poqo established power over Bantu settlements by means

[5]Quoted in Lauritz Strydom, Rivonia Unmasked. Johannesburg: Voortrekkerpers, 1965, p. 12.

of assaults and murders. In the Paarl District of the Western Cape toward the close of 1961, complete control over the Native township was secured by torturing those Bantu who refused to bow to *Poqo*'s will and, in some instances, by decapitating them while still alive.[6]

Throughout 1962, the terrorist campaign mounted in force. Three African policemen and a White businessman were clubbed and stabbed to death in Langa township during 1962–63. In November 1962, Rencia Vermeulen, an eighteen-year-old White girl, and her escort were hacked to death in Paarl. In October of the same year, an African tribal leader was murdered in the Transkei for cooperating with the authorities. For this, six *Poqo* members paid with their lives. A determined effort was made to assassinate Chief Minister Kaizer Matanzima of the Transkei, but the police rounded up *Poqo* murder teams #4 and #5. During 1962–63, the toll of *Poqo* crimes mounted—police sergeants hacked to death, White vacationers sleeping in tents and trailers attacked with gasoline bombs and, when they fled, hacked and knifed to death. The murder operations of *Poqo* were apparently indiscriminate where Whites were concerned and young girls of ten and fourteen were killed with characteristic savagery.

Robert Sobukwe, the leader of the Pan Africanist Congress, was in prison and *Poqo* was being run from Basutoland by his second-in-command, a certain Potlako Leballo. Boasting a membership of 150,000, Leballo promised an uprising for 1963 and made threatening statements concerning the imminent mass murder of men, women and children.[7]

[6]Chris Vermaak, *op. cit.* pp. 46–53. Vermaak gives a detailed and realistic account of *Poqo* crimes in contrast to pro-Communist writers, such as Mary Benson, who seek to portray these butchers as freedom fighters. [7]*Ibid.*, p. 50. Roux, *Time Longer Than Rope*, pp. 429–30.

On March 29, 1963, Leballo's African secretary was arrested near Ladybrand, carrying coded "battle orders" from Leballo to 150 cell leaders of the terrorist organization. "A wild dancing spree has been arranged for the night of April 8," the directive read. "On this night everyone must dance. . . ." The police moved swiftly, arresting 3,246 leaders and rank-and-file members. Included in the impressive arsenal of weapons seized were pangas, tomahawks, axes and needle-swords. The last is a two-foot circular steel rod, the piercing end of which is sharpened enough so that it can be plunged into a man's heart and withdrawn so rapidly that he dies without knowing what stabbed him.[8]

A month later, the British police in Basutoland raided PAC headquarters and seized the membership list of the organization. The 15,000 names on that roster became available to the South African police.

At about this time, Patrick Duncan, whose fame or notoriety was due less to anything he personally had accomplished than to the fact that his father had been Governor General of South Africa, renounced his belief in non-violence to become PAC's first White member. His house in Basutoland was made available to the PAC-*Poqo* leadership for the various activities of that organization. Early in 1964, Prime Minister Kaizer Matanzima accused Duncan before a meeting of the Legislative Assembly of inciting people to commit murder. Interviewed by Kenneth Alsop on the B.B.C. television "Tonight" program on June 15, 1963, Duncan predicted "an Algeria-type war in South Africa," adding that it would be "dreadful" and then implying that he would seek to minimize the ensuing "suffering and violence."[9]

---

[8]Vermaak, *op. cit.*, p. 51.
[9]*Ibid.*, p. 108.

As a Black nationalist movement, PAC had been at loggerheads with the Communists and had strongly disapproved of the multiracial character of South African Communism and of the fact that a small clique of White Communists dominated the African National Congress. These scruples did not, however, prevent Leballo from going to Red China in July 1964 and taking $10,000 from Mao's regime. A second pilgrimage to the Chinese People's Republic in February 1965 was followed by arrangements for training PAC activists in guerrilla warfare in Red Chinese military camps. The "close ties of solidarity" forged between PAC and Red China placed Patrick Duncan, who had been (or at least had claimed to be) a staunch anti-Communist, in an anomalous position.

The Rivonia Raid

In June 1963, the South African police were concerned over an "inaugural broadcast" by an underground radio station, which called itself Radio Liberation and claimed to be the voice of the banned African National Congress. Walter Sisulu, a former Secretary General of the African National Congress and a leading figure in the South African underground Communist Party, spoke over the clandestine transmitter and promised to "keep the freedom fight going" and "meet violence with violence."[10]

Shortly thereafter, the Security Branch of the South African National Police received a tip from an informant concerning a secret headquarters of the Communist Party at which Sisulu could be found. The police spent several days driving the informant around in search of a place with a sign reading "IVON" and a large house near a

[10]Strydom, *op. cit.*, p. 14.

church. The "church" turned out to be a gabled house and "IVON" to be the blurred, still legible letters of a sign reading "RIVONIA."

Rivonia is a wooded, wealthy residential area between Johannesburg and Pretoria, in which successful South African businessmen seek refuge from the bustle of urban life. In terms of architecture, terrain and income level, it is somewhat reminiscent of the Long Island Gold Coast. The purported Communist Party hideout was a 28-acre estate called Lilliesleaf with a large, rambling main house, a thatched cottage and four or five outbuildings.

Lilliesleaf posed immediate and obvious difficulties for the police. It was opulent enough to indicate trouble for the police if a surprise raid were launched and nothing incriminating found. Also, it was sufficiently large and sprawling to make the raiding technique of crucial importance. The police could assume that the occupants, if criminals, would have lookouts posted and would have time to burn documents and other evidence of their activities before a raiding party in prowl cars could enter the various buildings.

On the theory that the conspirators would work and move about by night and rest during daylight hours, a decision was taken to raid in the early afternoon. Sixteen detectives and policemen and a dog were packed into a dry-cleaning van, a vehicle calculated to arouse minimal interest or suspicion. A plainclothes policeman got out of the van, rang the front doorbell and, when a Bantu servant announced that nobody was at home, put his foot between the door and the jamb. The police officers in command gave the order to raid and the squad raced to get to the various buildings and their occupants before the latter could burn evidence.

The men swooped up in the Rivonia raid or picked up later because of evidence found in that raid included about half the top leadership of the illegal Party. Walter Sisulu, a small, light-skinned Negro with a Hitler moustache, was the man the police were most interested in finding. Self-educated, dedicated and intelligent, Sisulu was, at the time of his arrest, a member of the Center, or Central Committee of the Communist Party.[11] Govan Mbeki, a Bantu journalist in his early fifties, who would confess at his trial to acts of sabotage and preparations for armed revolution,[12] was also a Central Committee member. Another Negro defendant, Mhlaba, a 45-year-old messenger-clerk, served as a Communist courier on secret missions, and had been co-opted to the Center in 1963. A more important Bantu defendant was Nelson Mandela. Linked by documentary and other evidence to the Rivonia conspiracy, he was taken from prison to stand trial.

The one Indian defendant, Ahmed Mohammed Kathrada, had been seized at Rivonia while disguised by a dyed red beard and red hair. He stated proudly to the Court that he had been a Communist activist since the age of eleven, admitted to having attended international conferences in Czechoslovakia, Hungary and East Germany and stated that "anything" which non-Whites might do to gain their rights was justified.[13]

The White defendants were Dennis Goldberg, a civil engineer, who had served as commander in a Communist camp that trained young guerrillas in field communications and other skills necessary to effective partisan warfare,[14] and Lionel (Rusty) Bernstein, the only prisoner to be ac-

[11]Ludi and Grobbelaar, *op. cit.*, p. 39.
[12]Strydom, *op. cit.*, p. 134.
[13]*Ibid.*, p. 128.
[14]*Ibid.*, pp. 100–02.

quitted. A Johannesburg architect, Bernstein admitted to having been a Communist for 25 years, but successfully alleged that he had left the Party, without, however, changing his revolutionary convictions, when it was outlawed in 1950. A former leader of the Springbok Legion, the Red organization of veterans, Bernstein was actually a member of the Center at the time of his arrest.

Fifteen other persons—all of whom had left South Africa, were living within the country in illegality or were dead at the time of the trial—were named as co-conspirators in the indictment. Of these, three—Joe Slovo, Michael Harmel and P. Duma Nokwe—were members of the Central Committee. Among the other Red leaders implicated, Joe Slovo and his wife, Ruth First, had left the country for Britain in time to escape further attentions from the authorities; Bob Hepple had been arrested with the other Rivonia conspirators, but had escaped to Dar es Salaam by bribing a young prison guard; Michael Harmel had been named as a co-conspirator; and "Rusty" Bernstein, while acquitted, was immediately re-arrested under the 90-day detention law.

Operation Mayibuye

Mayibuye is a Zulu word meaning "return." *Operation Mayibuye* was a six-page typed blueprint for guerrilla warfare, armed invasion of South Africa and Communist conquest of that country. The significance of the title was "Return Africa to the Black Man."

The plan began by observing that the South African revolution could not be modelled after the Bolshevik Revolution of October 1917, in which by a concerted blow soldiers and workers seized Moscow and Petrograd, after which a struggle for possession of the rest of the country ensued. "Rather as in Cuba, the general uprising must be sparked off by organized and well-prepared guerrilla operations, during the course of which the masses of the people will be drawn in and armed."

The plan recognized that the internal South African forces on the side of revolution were weak in comparison with their enemy,

a powerfully armed, modern state with tremendous industrial resources, which can, at least in the initial period, count on the support of three million Whites. . . .

This state is isolated practically from the rest of the world, and if effective work is done will have to rely on the main on its own resources. . . . Direct military intervention in South West Africa, an effective economic and military boycott, even armed international action at some more advanced stage of the struggle are real possibilities which will play an important role. *In no other territory where guerrilla operations have been undertaken has the international situation been such a vital factor operating against the enemy.*[15] We are not unaware that there are powerful external monopoly interests who will attempt to bolster up the White state. With effective work they can be isolated and neutralized.

The following plan envisages a process which will place in the field, at a date fixed now, simultaneously in pre-selected areas, armed and trained guerrilla bands, who will find ready to join them local guerrilla bands with arms and equipment at their disposal. It will further coincide with a massive propaganda campaign both inside and outside South Africa, and a general call for unprecedented mass struggle throughout the land, both violent and non-violent. In the initial period, when for a short while the military advantage will be ours, the plan envisages a massive onslaught on pre-selected targets which will create maximum havoc and confusion in the enemy camp, and which will inject into the masses of the people and other friendly forces a feeling of confidence that here at last is the

[15]Emphasis supplied.

army of liberation equipped and capable of leading them to victory.[16]

The first revolutionary blow was to be struck in four key areas: Port Elizabeth-Mzimkulu, Port Shepstone-Swaziland, Northwestern Transvaal, bordering on Bechu-analand and the Limpopo River, and Northwestern Cape-South West Africa. Three of these regions offered secure lines of retreat for the revolutionary forces, in the event of defeat, into Black republics, protectorates or desert. The blow at the Transvaal, if successful, would have jeopardized Johannesburg and the gold mining industry of the Reef. The mandated territory of South West Africa was chosen for assault in order to stir up United Nations action to strip South Africa of her authority to govern the region.

The revolutionary movement was to be touched off with the simultaneous landing, by sea or air, of four groups of 30 men each, equipped with enough arms and provisions to be self-sustaining for a month. Each group was to split up into three independent platoons of 10 men each, which were to operate within specific areas in cooperation with previously alerted and trained local groups.

On landing, a detailed plan of attack on pre-selected targets with a view to taking the enemy by surprise, creating the maximum impact on the populace, creating as much chaos and confusion for the enemy as possible.

Choice of suitable areas will be based on the nature of the terrain, with a view to establishing temporary base areas from which our units can attack and to which they can retreat.

Before these operations take place political authority will have been set up in secrecy in a friendly territory with a view to supervising the struggle both in its internal and external aspects. It is visualized that this authority will in due course develop into a Provisional Revolutionary Government.

[16]Strydom, *op. cit.*, pp. 66–79, gives an excellent analysis of *Operation Mayibuye* in detail.

The political authority was to serve as a propaganda medium to press for worldwide, total boycott of South Africa, to enlist international trade union support, to use the United Nations as its chief sounding board, and to finance the revolutionary struggle by obtaining credits from sympathetic governments. It was to carry out daily propaganda broadcasts from its base of operations both to the outside world and to the people of South Africa. It was to be responsible for the organization of a weekly or bi-weekly air transport system to move in recruits, staff, military technicians and matériel of war and presumably to evacuate casualties.

In advance of the landings, 7,000 men in the target areas were to be trained, organized and readied to assist the platoons. These guerrilla-sabotage units were to "engage in activities that may serve to disperse the enemy forces, assist to maintain the fighting ability of the guerrillas as well as draw in the masses in support of the guerrillas."

The general staff of the revolution, referred to in the plan as the "National High Command of *Umkhonto We Sizwe*," was to operate from Dar es Salaam with complete authority in all military matters. The detailed plan involved five separate organizational fronts. *Intelligence* would have essentially the same functions as a divisional G-2 and in addition would have to pinpoint areas on the coast suitable for clandestine landings and report "the location of trading stations and chiefs' and headmen's *kraals.*"[17]

The *External Planning Committee* (or G-4) was to obtain the required arms, matériel of war and other supplies and to organize air, sea and land transport for the landing

[17]The trading posts were almost invariably run by Whites, and the Chiefs and Headmen were sympathetic to the South African authorities as a general rule. Presumably, those key people were marked for immediate liquidation.

forces. The *Political Authority* had the tasks already noted and in addition was to "set up a special committee to direct guerrilla political education." Finally the *Transport* and *Logistics Departments* had the function of equipping all forces in the field as the struggle gained in intensity.

The details of conducting guerrilla warfare were set forth in a seized document entitled "Speakers' Notes—A Brief Course of Training for Organizers," which begins with the statement: "You have been appointed to perform the important task of organizing units of *Umkhonto We Sizwe*" and proceeds with the observation that "the aims for which the war is being waged must be explained with absolute clarity, as it is imperative and vital that the people should understand and be convinced of the need to risk their lives for their ultimate freedom."

Operation Mayibuye was drafted by Arthur Goldreich, perhaps the most important of the men captured by the South African police at Rivonia. Unfortunately for the authorities, Goldreich managed to bribe his way out of prison. With a fellow escapee, Harold Wolpe, Goldreich made his way to the protectorate of Swaziland disguised as a priest. Thence they flew to Bechuanaland. The local population was thoroughly unsympathetic to the two terrorists and the plane that they had intended to take to Dar es Salaam, then as now a major operating base for Communist and Black Nationalist infiltrators into Rhodesia and South Africa, was blown up. Finally, Goldreich and Wolpe reached England. Due to the pressure on a reluctant British Government by the leftwing Labour Member of Parliament, Barbara Castle, they were permitted to remain in England for two months.[18]

---

[18]Mrs. Castle was President of the Anti-Apartheid Movement, a British organization heavily infiltrated by Communists, until her appointment as

During the trial, the absent Goldreich was referred to by Nelson Mandela and other defendants as a military expert who had served as an officer in the Israeli war for independence. Visa records indicate, however, that Goldreich was not in Israel at the time of the fighting.

Goldreich's plan is modelled on the guerrilla strategy of the Chinese Communists. A notebook in Goldreich's handwriting, seized at Rivonia, states: "First meeting with Chinese. Preliminary discussion on programme. Questions relating to Guerrilla warfare. List of technical questions. I study C.[19] Mao's works on strategy in prep. for discussion at Military Academy with military experts."[20] In Red China, Goldreich was given advanced training in the strategy and tactics of guerrilla warfare and the organization of partisan forces by Yang Ching and Lee of the People's Liberation Army. The fact that he was given no practical combat training in China suggests that he already had a basic military education.

Goldreich's notebook shows constant preoccupation with the practical details of the organization of revolutionary war. He goes into the types of explosives and fuses needed and their characteristics. In a discussion with a certain Comrade Manshisha (possibly an Algerian), he rejects transport of arms by sea on the grounds that transshipment on the high seas or clandestine unloading can easily be spotted and could cause diplomatic difficulties for the Communist government involved. He suggests that they

Minister of Overseas Development in the Labour Government. She helped arrange a press conference for Goldreich and Wolpe in London at which Goldreich repeated the usual propaganda line that he knew nothing of sabotage in South Africa and that his movement was not directed against Whites, but was a "freedom campaign" against "racial oppression."
[19]Chairman.
[20]Strydom, *op. cit.*, p. 114.

get their arms from friendly Black African states which would be compensated for the loss by the Soviets.[21] For the non-military supplies necessary for the civil war, such as radio parts and presses, Soviet equipment should be forwarded to the German Democratic Republic, which would in turn ship the material through normal commercial channels to South African consignees fronting for the Communists. "This question must be raised with German Comrades," he writes. "We must investigate how Soviet supplies can link up with German Comrades."

Using the pseudonym of Charles Barnard, Dennis Goldberg had bought a farm called Travallyn, which was to serve as the arsenal and engineering unit of the conspiracy. Here and in Goldreich's car, the police seized a document entitled *Production Requirements*. This specified 48,000 land mines, 210,000 hand grenades, 150 tons of ammonium nitrate, 20 tons of aluminum powder and 1,500 time fuses for bombs as needed for sabotage and the initial insurrectionary blow. Using still a different alias, Goldberg entered into correspondence with two lumber companies and requested quotations for enough shooks to manufacture 48,000 wooden boxes of the sort used to pack fruits and vegetables. The plan was to house the land mines in these boxes. They were to be buried in roadways, footpaths, gardens and entrances to private houses to liquidate people hostile to the revolution and to spread terror. They could also be transported by truck or rail to various parts of the country. Six months were allotted for procurement and production of the stockpiles listed in *Production Requirements*.[22]

[21]*Ibid.*, p. 113.
[22]*Ibid.*, pp. 75–76.

The Case of Bruno Mtolo

A Zulu Communist, who had been active in the sabotage campaign and in preparations for *Operation Mayibuye*, gave devastating testimony against the defendants in the Rivonia trial. To protect him against Red reprisals, he was identified only as Mr. X, but in 1966 he published his memoirs as a Communist under his real name—Bruno Mtolo.[23]

His reasons for defecting were revelatory. He wrote:

When our [sabotage] organization in Natal was formed, we were told that the moment one suspected that the police net was closing in on you, you had to report the matter to the Regional Command, so that you could be removed to a safe place, outside the country. When this happened to me and others, we were simply told to go underground, with no financial support of any kind. When the top leaders felt danger closing in on them, they ran. This instruction had obviously been only for the big shots and not for the small fry, who had to battle for themselves. . . .

The people who had formed the *Umkhonto We Sizwe* and who were involved had all run away. Only the small group which was rounded up at Rivonia was left. It cannot be said that this group stayed because they were prepared to carry on the fight for their ideals. In my opinion, they stayed only for the money which was pouring into the country. They thought they were quite safe where they were until the day came for them to have a dose of their own bitter aloes.

We, the poor fools, were left to nurse their baby. There is not the slightest indication that they were interested in the well-being of the African people as such. The guerrilla warfare which was to be launched by the fools who were left behind would have been a failure in a country like South Africa, where

[23]Bruno Mtolo, *Umkhonto We Sizwe, the Road to the Left*. Durban: Drakensberg Press, 1966.

there are no thick bushes and where the methods of communication are first class. . . . What would probably have happened if these plans were carried out successfully is that the United Nations "peace force" would have taken over in South Africa. The same things that came about in the Congo would have happened here.[24]

Mtolo had been promised a small monthly salary and a meager allowance for his wife and small children who lived in the Zulu tribal territories. The High Command never gave his family anything. Although Mtolo had given up his permanent job to work for the Party and had no other resources, the High Command paid him only 10 rand ($14.00) between his recruitment for sabotage in June 1962 and his arrest a year later. When asked by Prosecutor Percy Yutar whether the leaders fared better, Mtolo retorted bitterly: "Mlangeni had a motor car. Walter Sisulu was able to pay R6,000 bail—six thousand rand. And after he had paid the six thousand, he still had his car. When I had to go into hiding, nobody cared if my children went hungry. They did not even pay the rent of my room which was R3 a month."[25]

The final straw was a conversation he had while in prison with an Afrikaner guard, who asked him: "Let us say you have a daughter, would you like to have a European or an Indian as a son-in-law?"

Even though he had attended multiracial Communist meetings and parties, Mtolo's reaction was:
. . . never mind about my daughter marrying a White man or an Indian—I just cannot imagine myself having Coloured kids. Neither could I imagine myself having a wife whose parents I could not visit and feel at home with. She would feel the same about my parents. . . . The situation is worse among the Zulus,

24Ibid., pp. 153–54.
25Strydom, op. cit., p. 93.

who do not even recognize the other Black tribes as their equals. . . . Likewise with the Xhosa. They regard everyone who is not a Xhosa as someone whose brain is not ripe enough, not to mention Indians or Whites.[26]

Mtolo testified to having been instructed in how to handle dynamite by co-defendant Jack Hodgson, to having been to Rivonia, to having conferred with such members of the High Command as Joe Slovo, Kathrada and Sisulu, and to having been given sabotage orders for Natal by Mbeki. He and his associates had planted a bomb in the office of the Security Staff in Durban, had tried to burn down the office of an unsympathetic Indian named Kajee and had tried to destroy the Coloured Affairs Department office by fire. Another Communist had placed a bomb in a third-class railway coach and had narrowly escaped killing three hundred passengers, most of them non-Europeans.[27]

The witness, the most important of the 173 persons who gave testimony at the Rivonia trial, explained how the High Command ordered the African National Congress to organize 200 recruits for military training abroad by August 1963. Trainees were flown from Francistown to Dar es Salaam and thence shipped to such countries as Ethiopia, Algeria, the Soviet satellite states, Cuba, and Red China for military training. Many of these men were persuaded to volunteer for advanced education abroad and discovered they were to serve as infiltrators and terrorists only when it was too late to back out.

The Enigma of Nelson Mandela

In the summer of 1962, Mtolo was summoned to a secret meeting to hear the report of Nelson Mandela who

[26]Mtolo, *op. cit.*, pp. 139–40.
[27]*Ibid.*, p. 47.

had just returned from a tour of Black African states and had collected R60,000 from them for the revolutionary struggle in South Africa. Mandela told the group how he had been received by the commander-in-chief of the Algerian armed forces, a Communist or Communist sympathizer, shown a guerrilla training camp and promised that South African recruits would be sent there to be trained and given the arms they needed.[28] Emperor Haile Selassie of Ethiopia had been equally sympathetic and had made similar promises. Cuba would accept guerrilla recruits and East Germany would train military engineers and radio men.

All this was confirmed by Mandela's diary, which was produced at the trial. In the Black African states, Mandela was considered a Government guest and "treated very lavishly" by such leaders as Julius Nyerere, Haile Selassie, Habib Bourguiba, Sekou Touré, Léopold Senghor, Ben Bella of Algeria and William Tubman of Liberia. He received money for the cause from Nigeria, Tunisia, Morocco, Liberia and Ethiopia and promises from Senegal and the Sudan. In London, he was able to meet such eminent politicians as Hugh Gaitskell, leader of the Labour Party, and Jo Grimond, leader of the Liberals.

Nelson Rolihlahla Mandela was the son of a Tembuland tribal chieftain of the Xhosa. Educated at Fort Hare University College, he was an attorney by profession and a revolutionary politician by avocation. He was able to meet chiefs of state and leaders of British political parties because of the Establishment view that Black leaders were idealistic nationalists dedicated to creating brave, progressive emerging nations. He was characterized by the liberal and crypto-Communist enemies of South Africa in

[28]Strydom, *op. cit.* p. 87.

such hyperbolic terms as "the Black Pimpernel" and "a major politician of vision and humanity."[29] The fact that he was a member of the Center of the outlawed Communist Party of South Africa was studiously ignored or categorically denied despite the fact that a tendentious document in his handwriting was produced at the Rivonia trial entitled *How To Be a Good Communist*.[30] In his diary, this "politician of vision and humanity" had stressed the necessity of ruthlessly eliminating informers and had advocated "cutting off their noses, *pour encourager les autres.*"[31]

For the Bantu members of *Operation Mayibuye*, the leader was not Slovo or Goldreich, but Nelson Mandela.[32] Shortly after his meeting with Mtolo, Mandela was arrested by Security Police in Natal and sentenced to five years' imprisonment. He was brought from prison to the dock at Rivonia and, at the conclusion of that trial, sentenced to a life term.

The manner of his arrest is something of an enigma. Bartholomew Hlapane, one of the few Bantu members of the Communist Party Center to survive the Rivonia affair, later turned against the Party. At the trial of Fred Carneson, an old-time White Communist and member of the Center,[33] Hlapane testified concerning the alleged treachery of White Communists toward their Black associates. Whether true or not, his statements illustrated the strong

[29]Nelson Mandela, *No Easy Walk to Freedom*. London: Heinemann, 1965. The quotation is from the dust jacket blurb.

[30]Mandela testified that he had not written the document; it consisted, he alleged, of notes he had made on lectures by an unnamed friend who had tried to convert him to Communism! It contained such statements as: "In our country, the struggle of the oppressed masses is led by the South African Communist Party and inspired by its policy."

[31]Strydom, *op. cit.*, p. 107.

[32]v. Mtolo, *op. cit.*, pp. 32–42.

[33]He was sentenced to five years' imprisonment.

undercurrent of hostility between the two groups. Hlapane said:

One has got to be honest and I say it is the White Communists who are dishonest. Fred Carneson himself gave evidence against Walter Sisulu in 1963, and Walter Sisulu got six years for that. And I can also say that it is through the White Communists that Nelson Mandela got arrested and also got a sentence before the Rivonia trial. Following Mandela's return from abroad, he reported to the Central Committee of the Communist Party that the African States were not prepared to support the African people as long as they worked together with the Whites—with the Communist Party; that they were prepared to back the struggle of the African people financially and otherwise, but only if we broke away from the Whites. If we did not break away, they were not prepared to do a thing for us.

After this report was given to the Central Committee, the feeling was that Nelson Mandela failed to defend Communism abroad. It was whispered that he was becoming a Pan-Africanist, along the lines of Robert Sobukwe. As such, he was told to sit down and it was suggested that he be disciplined.

Mandela replied, according to Hlapane, that "we have got to come to a breaking point" and that he intended to report to his own people the true attitude of the Black African states toward the South African revolutionary movement. Mandela's decision sealed his fate because the Party felt that "he must not be allowed to report to his people what the African states thought about us." After Mandela had been arrested, Hlapane continued, Lionel (Rusty) Bernstein told the Central Committee that Mandela was "an ambitious, undisciplined, reckless young man," who "is now in jail and he can rot in jail. . . ."

Before his report to the Central Committee, Mandela had been given full protection by the Communist Party through *Umkhonto We Sizwe*, from Johannesburg right up to Lobatsi, Bechuanaland. The whole road was lined by people who were fully armed to see to the protection of Mandela. They had instructions to shoot on the spot to kill if they met any obstruction. But after giving his report to the Central Committee and when Mandela proceeded to Durban to report to his people, he was denied the same protection. The Central Committee said he would be given a car and a driver, but no protection. He was told: "If you get into trouble, it is your own look-out."

And, in fact, it is today known in Communist Party circles that there were people who were prepared to testify that certain women deliberately gave information about Nelson Mandela's visit to Durban. They felt that a commission of inquiry should be instituted into the betrayal. This was suppressed by the Communist Party whose White members had betrayed Mandela. . . .[34]

Verdict and World Opinion

In a 72-page verdict, Mr. Justice De Wet found Mandela, Sisulu, Goldberg, Mbeki, Mhlaba, Motsoaledi and Mlangeni guilty of recruiting persons for training in sabotage and guerrilla warfare to cause insurrection in South Africa, of specific acts of sabotage, of having promoted the ends of Communism and of having collected and spent funds for purposes of sabotage. The judge dismissed the charge that the defendants had conspired to wage guerrilla warfare and to provide military assistance to invaders of South Africa on the grounds that the state had not proved that the accused had decided to carry out *Operation Mayibuye*.[35] Kathrada was convicted on one count only. Lionel Bernstein was acquitted on the basis of insufficient evi-

---

[34]Vermaak, *op. cit.*, pp. 101–03.
[35]The defendants claimed they had abandoned *Operation Mayibuye* as impractical.

dence. The eight convicted defendants were sentenced to serve terms of imprisonment for life.

There was the expected clerical support for the convicted saboteurs and terrorists. Canon L. John Collins, Chairman of Christian Action and, incidentally, also head of the British "Ban the Bomb" movement, was the most prominent and influential of these people. Christian Action had a Defence and Aid Fund. Hlapane testified in the Braam Fischer trial that money for the South African Communist Party was channeled through this fund, and Doreen Tucker, a Johannesburg administrator of the Fund, admitted that she supposed she knew she "was working for the Communist Party."[36] Canon Collins was on a first-name basis with such Communist underground leaders of sabotage and terrorism as Sisulu and Fischer. In 1965, Canon Collins told the United Nations Special Committee on Apartheid that he needed funds "for the purpose of supporting the underground resistance movement in South Africa." In that same year, Collins' Defence and Aid Fund was declared an unlawful organization under the South African Suppression of Communism Act. The extent to which the dry rot of totalitarianism had infected the Christian clergy in South Africa was revealed in Canon Collins' 1966 book, *Faith under Fire,* where he revealed that, at a 1964 conference of 40 Anglican priests, 39 produced membership cards in the Communist-controlled African National Congress.[37]

On October 12, 1963, the United States supported a United Nations resolution demanding that South Africa free all her political prisoners. The resolution referred specifically to "the arbitrary trial now in progress." The Secu-

[36]Vermaak, *op. cit.,* pp. 68–69.
[37]*Ibid.,* p. 73.

rity Council proceeded to "demand" amnesty for those who had been condemned to death or were suffering in prisons "for having opposed Apartheid." South Africa's then Minister of Justice (and later Prime Minister) B. J. Vorster explained that nobody in South Africa is sentenced to death for opposition to the Government's policies, provided that opposition does not take the form of bomb throwing or assassination. The explanation fell on ears that had become deaf because they heard only what they wished to hear.

The press of South Africa, with a majority in opposition to the Nationalist Government, judged the Rivonia trial fair and the verdict just. The leader of the United Party, the official opposition to the Government, supported the verdicts in Parliament.

"I want to say quite clearly," Sir De Villiers Graaf observed on that occasion,

that we of the Opposition want it on record, so that not only this House will know but that the outside world will know too, that we are convinced that the verdicts in that trial were just, that they were necessary and that they were right in view of the actions to which the accused themselves pleaded guilty. Those findings were arrived at by one of South Africa's great judges, a man who has proved himself not only a learned jurist, but a wise man. In his judgment, he pointed out that these men were guilty of treasonable activity. I want to say that if I have any regret, then my only regret is that they were not charged with high treason.[38]

Four days after the Rivonia sentences, Prime Minister Hendrik F. Verwoerd said:

We were dealing here with a Communist attack which was directed not only against South Africa but against the West. . . .

[38]Strydom, *op. cit.*, pp. 162–163.

When there is a revolt in Cuba, people are caught and immediately shot; or when there is a revolt in Zanzibar, death follows. . . . In spite of that, the Western powers continue to have diplomatic relations with them, first with the one government, then with the rebel government. They do not worry about what happens in regard to the domestic affairs of those countries. Why is different treatment meted out to South Africa? Only in the case of an anti-Communist country like South Africa, where a revolt is suppressed, do we get this world-wide organized propaganda. . . .

. . . I ask the Western world at least to look after its own interests and to realize that if South Africa were to fall prey to Communist conspiracies, the West would suffer also. Even if the West assists in making us fall prey by trying, in the atmosphere which prevails, to gain the friendship and support of everybody else at the cost of South Africa, it should bear in mind that, if a conquered South Africa becomes Communist, the noose about the neck of Europe and America will only be drawn tighter. It will not only be the end of us, but also the beginning of the end for them. When therefore it is said in those circles that they are glad that Mandela received a life sentence and not the death sentence, because he may still, like Kenyatta, become the leader of the future, then I say, "God forbid!" If that were to happen, not only would South Africa be doomed and become Communist, but then the world would in time be conquered by Communism, because after that the only bastions which still protect White civilization against that pernicious ideology would fall one after another.[39]

[39]*Ibid.*, pp. 163–164.

❖ ❖ ❖ ❖ ❖

CHAPTER TEN

Braam Fischer and the Red Underground

" 'The masses are advancing,' said Hegel in apocalyptic fashion. 'Without some new spiritual influence, our age, which is a revolutionary age, will produce a catastrophe,' was the pronouncement of Comte. 'I see the flood-tide of nihilism rising,' shrieked Nietzsche from a crag of the Engadine. It is false to say that history cannot be foretold. Numberless times this has been done. If the future offered no opening to prophecy, it could not be understood when fulfilled in the present and on the point of falling back into the past."

—JOSÉ ORTEGA Y GASSET, *The Revolt of the Masses*[1]

EARLY IN AUGUST 1963, BRAAM FISCHER HELD A MEETING of leading Communists in Bellevue, Johannesburg, to survey the wreckage of the Party after Rivonia. The Central Committee had been reduced to two persons—Ruth First, the able wife of Joe Slovo, and himself. Mrs. First was about to leave for Britain to join her husband and raise

[1]New York: W. W. Norton & Company, 25th printing, 1957. Originally, *La Rebelión de las Masas*, 1930.

money for South African Communist activities. Reported Fischer:

That means that the Central Committee will consist of only one person—myself. Now that is impossible, comrades. We must start all over again. The rest of the Central Committee fell into the Rivonia net and, as you know, many of our comrades fled the country. A new Central Committee will have to be formed immediately to continue the struggle. Although there have been enormous losses all over the country, a considerable part of our internal organization remains intact. This applies particularly in the Transvaal, where our own and Congress machinery operates on various levels.

Despite "all our grievous errors and despite so much betrayal," Fischer continued, "whole areas of activity and equipment . . . have been completely untouched by the police." Rebuilding the underground Party, finding safe ways to operate, and training new cadres were the urgent tasks of the moment.

The cardinal errors committed by the Party in Braam Fischer's opinion had been to have underestimated the police, to have held "too many meetings far too long in the same places," to have left documents and other incriminating evidence lying around, to have functioned without adequate cover and to have recruited without sufficient security checks.[2]

The decisive weapon which had destroyed the Communist Party, Fischer indicated, was the 90-day detention

[2]*Time for Reassessment,* a Communist Party document by Fischer, quoted in Chris Vermaak, *Braam Fischer, the Man with Two Faces.* Johannesburg: APB Publishers, 1966, pp. 87–90. The writer has the text of this and other seized Communist Party documents. However, to cite the document itself, which is unavailable to the general reader, and to fail to cite secondary sources in which it can be obtained seem mere pedantry of the most useless sort.

clause of the 1963 General Laws Amendment Bill. This
was one of several measures that the new Minister of
Justice, Balthazar John Vorster, had successfully proposed
to Parliament in 1962 and 1963 to crush Communism. It
gave the Minister of Justice authority to detain people suspected of subversive activity in solitary confinement for 90
days without trial. The detained persons were to be released
when they had answered in a satisfactory manner all questions put to them. Failing this, they could be re–arrested
and again placed in solitary. In practice, the harshness of
this measure was somewhat mitigated by requiring review
of the evidence against suspects by senior officials of the
National Police, most of them lawyers, before they could
be detained. Ninety-day solitary confinement imposed terrible psychological strains even on seasoned Communist
militants. It was impossible to predict who would break
under the strain and who would weather the ordeal. The
result was that Communists who had served a 90-day
sentence would be considered an unknown quantity and
often isolated and treated as potential traitors.[3]

"Our second principal error," Braam Fischer told the
meeting,

was that we failed completely to understand the power of the
90-day detention weapon when it was applied by cruel, ruth-
less and often clever men.

To resist torture, people must be strong and brave, and must
prepare themselves in advance to withstand it by realising what
lies ahead of them if they are arrested: by preparing themselves

[3]Other security measures adopted because of Communist and *Poqo* sabotage, terrorism and murder included 24-hour house arrest; making it an
offense for banned persons to associate with each other unless married;
requiring some to report daily to the police; and prohibiting others from
having visitors, preparing material for publication or having their writings
published.

mentally and resolving not to answer questions or make statements under any circumstances. We also failed to examine
methods of eliciting information from people which are not
new or original to South Africa, but standard police practice
throughout the world. Because the police had shown themselves ignorant and stupid in the past, we did not even bother
to study such practices.

There are certain methods of interrogation, for example play-
ing one person against another, using the "sympathetic, kindly"
investigator after the crude, cruel one; confronting the victim
with isolated bits of information that appear to show someone
else has given the whole thing away; irregularity of ways and
times of questioning, thus causing uncertainty and confusion,
and other methods that people could better withstand if they
knew in advance what to expect. . . .

Many freedom fighters have behaved in an exemplary way. . . .
Others gave way. Some gave, but gave the minimum, resisting
as much as possible and concealing a great deal. Others made
restitution by refusing to give evidence against their own comrades. Others gave way and volunteered statements to save
their skins.

To their unending shame, this cowardly conduct has led to
numerous arrests, detentions and long-term jail sentences. It
may even lead to sentence of death on those with whom they
formerly worked. The names of such people, too, will go down
in history. Even if they appear to go free now, their punishment will be far greater than any prison sentence.[4]

A new Central Committee, consisting, in the main, of
secondary leaders, was constituted. Of the new group,
which was preponderantly White, the most interesting
additions were Petrus Byleveld, the Afrikaner ex-leader of
the Sprinkbok Legion, and Hlapane, the Bantu who was
to cast such interesting light on the background of the
arrest and possible betrayal of Nelson Mandela.

[4]Vermaak, *op. cit.*, pp. 90–91.

Ninety-Day Detention and Due Process

Ninety-day detention was denounced by international liberal opinion with customary hyperbole as a barbarous institution, repugnant to all traditions of Anglo-Saxon law and reminiscent of Nazi Germany. A more restrained and valid critique of the law was that of the distinguished South African liberal political scientist, Leo Marquard. "The law inhibits discretion," Marquard wrote, "and society must be governed by laws as opposed to the discretion of individuals. The rule of law implies a number of things: that a man is innocent until proved guilty; that the onus of proof must not rest on the defendant; above all, that laws must be administered by an independent judiciary."

Marquard conceded that

a deviation from the rule of law may be justified in an emergency situation, but the emergency powers must be limited in time and the jurisdiction of the courts must not be excluded. In the United States, for example, the State may act in an emergency but it must subsequently be able to prove in court that there was "a clear and present danger." Under the 90-day clause in South Africa, the jurisdiction of the courts is excluded and discretion rests solely with the Minister of Justice. That, clearly, is contrary to the rule of law.[5]

There is no controversy about the inconsistency between the 90-day detention clause and due process of law. The question is whether the United States and other indubitably democratic countries offer greater safeguards in time of national emergency. Here, the historic record is neither unambiguous nor simple. Article I, Section 9, Clause 2 of

[5]Leo Marquard, *Liberalism in South Africa.* Johannesburg: South African Institute of Race Relations, 1965, p. 16–17.

the Constitution reads: "The Privilege of the Writ of Habeas Corpus shall not be suspended, unless when in Cases of Rebellion or Invasion the public Safety may require it."

In the Civil War, President Lincoln, acting under this power, arrested and incarcerated tens of thousands of people whose loyalty was suspect, denying them *habeas corpus* and holding them without specific accusations of crime. When Chief Justice of the United States Roger B. Taney ordered that one of these arrested suspects appear before him, Lincoln replied that he had authorized the Commanding General ". . . to arrest and detain, without resort to the ordinary processes and forms of law, such individuals as he might deem dangerous to the public safety. . . . Are all the laws, *but one*, to go unexecuted, and the government itself go to pieces, lest that one be violated?"

Unlike South Africa a century later, Lincoln had acted by executive fiat without congressional authority. On this point, he told Taney: "Now it is insisted that Congress, and not the Executive, is vested with this power. But the Constitution, itself, is silent as to which, or who, is to exercise the power. . . ."[6]

What Lincoln's biographer, Carl Sandburg, called "the terror of secret and arbitrary arrests" continued to reign during the war years.[7] After the storm of civil conflict had subsided, a sharply divided Supreme Court held that Lincoln had acted unlawfully and that martial law could not prevail "*after* the (civil) courts are reinstated."[8] But this decision did not influence or restrain the conduct of the United States Government during the Civil War itself and

[6]Lincoln to Taney, July 4, 1861. Carl Sandburg, *Abraham Lincoln*. New York: Harcourt, Brace & Company, one-volume edition, 1954, pp. 247–48.
[7]*Ibid.*, p. 373.
[8]*Ex parte Milligan*, 4 Wall. 2 (1866).

it is doubtful whether its precedent would serve as restraint in a future American crisis of that magnitude.

South Africa was abused by international liberal opinion for her 90-day detention clause, although the British authorities in Kenya had suspended *habeas corpus* during the Mau Mau troubles for a period of years without arousing the interest or comment of the outside world. When the Indian defendant, Kathrada, took the stand at the Rivonia trial and protested the 90-day detention clause, Prosecutor Yutar asked him whether he knew that "in India there is a law under which persons can be detained for three years without trial."[9] Few of the liberals who assailed South Africa's comparatively mild measures of self-defense had protested the Soviet and East European procedure of arresting suspects without any semblance of due process and sending them to prison camps in which an estimated 20 million died.[10] Nor had their consciences been disturbed over the fact that as late as 1954 Latvian and Ukrainian women prisoners at Kingur labor camp were crushed by tanks when they protested conditions.[11]

Braam Fischer

Abram (Braam) Fischer was the scion of one of South Africa's most distinguished Afrikaner families. His grandfather, Abraham Fischer, had been sent to Europe during the Anglo-Boer War to raise money for the Orange Free State and the Transvaal. After the Peace of Vereeniging in 1902, he served with distinction as Prime Minister of the reconstituted Orange Free State and took part in the National Convention at which the Union of South Africa

[9]Strydom, *op. cit.*, p. 127.
[10]Robert Conquest, *The Great Terror*. New York: Macmillan, 1968, p. 533.
[11]*Ibid.*, p. 516.

was formed. His son, Peter Ulrich Fischer, became Judge-President of Orange Free State in the 1930's. Peter Ulrich's eldest son, Braam Fischer, was a brilliant student in school and at the University of Cape Town, an outstanding athlete and a champion of segregation who detested "British imperialism." After serving as prime minister of the University Parliament, Braam got his law degree and earned a Rhodes scholarship, which sent him to Oxford in 1932.

He associated with leftists at Oxford and the London School of Economics, toured Eastern Europe, visited Moscow and returned to South Africa a student of Marxism-Leninism and a fervent integrationist.[12] Despite the fact, that he was known as a parlor Communist, Braam Fischer became a King's Counsellor before the age of forty and was soon recognized as one of the outstanding trial lawyers in the nation. When the Congress of Democrats was launched to substitute for the open Communist Party that had been outlawed in 1950, Braam Fischer emerged as its leader. To South African professionals and intellectuals, Fischer was a prominent leftwing spokesman for peace causes; to the South African National Police, he was the directing brain behind the illegal Communist Party and the man chiefly responsible for organizing the epidemic of sabotage that broke out in the early 1960's.[13]

Braam Fischer was one of the chief attorneys for the

[12]Vermaak, *op. cit.*, preface. He carried his views on racial equality to such an extent that he allowed a Bantu servant to interrupt a speech he gave to the Transvaal Peace Council with the observation: "Come now, Braam, you are talking too much." He adopted the child of another African servant to prove that, given an equal environment, the Bantu would develop mentally and morally like Whites. The experiment was terminated when the teenage adopted girl, Nora, became pregnant by a Bantu taxi driver. The cab driver paid *lobola* (bride price) to Fischer and married the girl.

[13]Only the most naive South African police officers suspected former Zulu Chief Albert Luthuli of masterminding these operations. Most Afrikaner police assumed that the directing brain belonged to a White man. Vermaak, *op. cit.*, p. 11.

defendants at Rivonia. Dr. Percy Yutar, the prosecutor, had asked all the accused who had testified to identify the top leader of the South African Communist Party, but they refused to answer. The suspicion that the man was Braam Fischer was reinforced by an article by Lionel (Rusty) Bernstein, supposedly destined to be Propaganda Commissar of a future South African Communist regime, in the suppressed periodical, *Fighting Talk*, for September 1953, which was an unrestrained encomium on Fischer.[14]

Cells of the Underground Party

A month or so before the Rivonia raid, Gerard Ludi, a 24-year-old tall, thin young man with a goatee, who had been active in the Congress of Democrats and had attended interracial sex parties, was approached by Jean Strachan, an activist in the underground, and asked to join the Party. Ludi, who was an undercover agent of the South African police, replied truthfully: "That has been my desire all along." Ludi was instructed by Strachan in the paramount importance of secrecy, told always to use code names for comrades, always to refer to the illegal Party as the Family or the Office, to observe strict discipline and to test the loyalty of potential recruits. Dues were from 1 per cent of the pay of the poorer comrades to over 10 per cent for those making more than $560 monthly.

At a cell meeting on December 23, 1964, a majority of

[14]The article read in part: "Braam . . . has all the attributes which go to make a cabinet minister or diplomat: personality which attracts people to him and makes him the most popular and best-liked figure in whatever circle he moves: powerful connections, both in his own right and through his wife with the family of J. C. Smuts: a tremendous capacity for conscientious and painstaking work, coupled with a keen and logical mind." Dr. Yutar believed that Nelson Mandela was destined to be Deputy Prime Minister and Defense Minister of the Revolutionary Government and that Luthuli would figurehead as its President.

the six members urged that the witnesses for the State at the Rivonia trial be shot. A certain Trewhela proposed that the Party set up a "revolutionary trial body" for the purpose and a bloodthirsty female Communist named Sylvia Neame added: "We must have one Justice Kuper a week." The allusion was to a judge who had been murdered by an unknown assailant after sentencing a Communist to three years' imprisonment.[15] These proposals were forwarded to the next higher Party echelon for decision.

The Noose Around Braam Fischer

On June 12, 1964, the convicted non-European defendants of the Rivonia trial were flown to Robben Island to begin life sentences. With his wife, Molly, and three of their children, Braam Fischer drove to Cape Town to explore the possibilities of appeal. The car, with Braam at the wheel, plunged over an embankment and landed in a stream. Fischer and his children escaped uninjured, but Molly drowned.

Brigadier General Hendrik van den Bergh, the head of the Security Branch and the man responsible for crushing Communism in South Africa, decided to trap Fischer by making it appear to his comrades that he was a traitor who was working hand in glove with the police. Fischer was obtrusively followed by police agents and, at one point, his car was stopped and searched for incriminating evidence, after which it was allowed to proceed. A Security Branch informer inside the ranks of the Party then began to spread the story that Braam Fischer was a broken man, shaken both by the death of his wife and by the destruc-

[15]Vermaak, op. cit., pp. 131–36.

tion of the Party that he had worked so hard to build. Knowing that the police had enough evidence to destroy him, Braam had decided to turn informer. His car had been searched to give Braam an opportunity to pass reports to the police. Moreover, shortly after his return to Johannesburg, Fischer would be arrested by the Security Police and detained for three days. This would be a bluff to cover up conferences between Braam and the authorities.

Braam's arrest and release were timed to corroborate the denunciation by the infiltrator. Meanwhile, an electronic device was picking up a conversation between comrades Jean Strachan and Anne Nicholson concerning Braam Fischer. The Fischers, Jean Strachan declared, "have the seeds of nationalism—Afrikaner nationalism—in them; small traces of it, you know. Like Nelson Mandela has got small traces of something else in him."[16]

Three months later, on September 23, 1964, Fischer was arrested in his law offices. Thirteen other members of the Communist underground, five of them from the Party cell Ludi had infiltrated, stood in the dock with Braam when the trial opened in November.

Over the strong objections of the prosecution, the trial judge granted Fischer bail of R10,000 to enable him to travel to London to appear before the British Privy Council in an appellate case. Both the authorities and a large part of public opinion assumed Fischer would never return to South Africa. In London, he was lionized by the Left. In addition to handling his trial work, he had long conferences with the Overseas Committee of the South African Communist Party on such matters as security, courier

[16]*Ibid.*, p. 144.

communications, finances and the reoganization of the Party in general to meet the new conditions of struggle.

To the amazement of many, Fischer returned to South Africa. He became something of an international hero and audiences throughout the world were told that here was a supposed Communist who lived according to his code of honor.[17] The true significance of the dramatic return was that Braam believed he could beat down the prosecution and win a dramatic acquittal.

Braam's first disagreeable shock was the appearance of Petrus Byleveld as a witness for the prosecution. An Afrikaner from the Orange Free State, the 48-year-old Byleveld had been a farmer until his enlistment in World War II. After V-J Day, Byleveld worked with the Springbok Legion, then joined the Congress of Democrats and in time became its President, and, at one time, also served as President of the South African Congress of Trade Unions. Recruited into the Communist Party in 1956, he was a member of its Central Committee at the time of the Fischer trial. This dedicated Marxist-Leninist had fallen into the trap set by the Security Branch and convinced himself that Braam Fischer planned to betray the Party to save his own skin. "I have failed as a Communist," he testified at the Fischer trial.

While Gerard Ludi's was more a worm's-eye view of South African Communism, he had the advantage of being a trained agent, working in close cooperation with the Security Branch. As Secret Agent Q-018, Ludi had compiled 600 reports to the police during four years. He testified concerning proposals by Nicholson and Trewhela that arson should be attempted, traitors liquidated and isolated

[17]Vermaak, *op. cit.*, p. 160.

police posts wiped out. Working through the surviving front organizations, the Party was concentrating on dramatizing the "psychological torture" of 90-day detention and urging a national-democratic revolution "to establish a non-racial social-democratic state." Ludi added that, after this had been achieved, "the Communist Party would actively work for a *coup d'etat* by the Party to establish a Communist state as soon as possible."[18]

The Odyssey of Braam Fischer

When the trial session of January 26, 1965, opened, Braam Fischer's chair was vacant. He had sneaked out of his house the preceding Sunday, leaving letters for his daughter and his attorney. When he learned Fischer had absconded, Prosecutor J. H. Liebenberg stated: "I must control my language while speaking about the incident. Fischer's deed is that of a coward."[19]

Fischer's letter of explanation was in part a leftwing assault on South African policies of the sort that had become familiar. But it also contained an interesting attempted personal justification of his act and a retort to the predictable charge that he was a coward who had deserted his comrades in the dock. "I realize fully that my eventual punishment may be increased by my present conduct," Fischer declared, adding: "I have not taken this step lightly. As you will no doubt understand, I have experienced great conflict between my desire to stay with my fellow accused and, on the other hand, to try to continue the political work that I believe essential."

Fischer predicted that "appalling bloodshed and civil

18Ludi and Grobbelaar, *op. cit.*, p. 67.
19*Ibid.*, p. 70.

war" would inevitably ensue in South Africa because "as long as there is oppression of a majority, such oppression will be fought with increasing hatred."

He claimed that his reason for flight was to encourage by his example "even some people to think about, to understand and to abandon the policies they now so blindly follow." Stating that he could no longer "serve justice" as he had over the past 30 years,[20] he asked the Court, in sentencing his comrades, to remember that "it will be punishing them for holding the ideas today that will be universally accepted tomorrow."[21]

A main purpose of this ingenious document was to perpetuate the myth of Braam Fischer as an altruist and hero who had placed himself on the sacrificial altar to inspire more liberal policies in his native land. The conclusion that the public might reach without Braam's rhetoric, namely, hat Communists were people actuated solely by revolutionary expediency, whose word of honor was worthless, was to be avoided. It is a safe inference that Fischer absconded when and only when he realized that the prosecution had inside witnesses whose testimony would almost certainly convict him.

Despite the fact that Fischer's disappearance was a nationwide sensation, the Security Branch did little or nothing during the first several weeks to try to apprehend him. General van den Bergh assumed that Fischer's preparations had been methodical and that any such attempt would probably be a waste of time and manpower. If it could safely be assumed that Fischer had fled in order to lead the Communist Party from illegality, then, in due

[20]In claiming that he had served justice, Fischer was referring to his activities as an attorney.
[21]v. Ludi and Grobbelaar, *op. cit.*, pp. 70–71 for the full text.

time, he could be found through surveillance of known or suspected Reds still at large. Once found, his activities could be watched for a long enough time so that virtually the entire underground organization would fall into the net. This analysis and decision required Security Branch leadership of great firmness and a willingness to risk bitter public criticism for inaction in case it proved wrong.

Meanwhile, Miss Gabrielle Fredericka Veglio di Castelleto, a 23-year-old student at Witwatersrand University, received a major and flattering assignment. A reliable but unimportant cog in the Communist movement known as "Comrade Ann," she was ordered to tell the manager of the Stock Exchange Branch of Barclay's Bank that she had just received a legacy, to open an account there, to learn to forge the signature of the cover name used in that account exactly, and to deposit the £6,000 that had just been received for the underground from the Overseas Committee of the Communist Party in London. Using this bank account, she rented a house in Waverley, Johannesburg, paying her rent in advance, and bought a Volkswagen.

Having made all these preparations, "Comrade Ann" let it be known that she had to return to England because of an ailing mother, but had arranged to have a middle-aged man named Douglas Black take over the premises and the car.

The new occupant of the house in Waverley was bald with bandy legs and methodical habits—a retired professor probably, his neighbors thought. He had gone about the business of disguising himself by using an electric needle to burn out hair roots on his forehead until the hairline had receded an inch and a half. The same procedure changed the shape of his eyebrows. He had added to his lean and gaunt appearance by a strict regimen of exercise and diet that took pounds off his frame. Perhaps for security reasons and perhaps because the Party had no such contact, Braam Fischer had not gone to a plastic surgeon, but had engineered the metamorphosis himself and in solitude.

He made the mistake of growing a beard to conceal a scar on his lip. Since beards were uncommon in South Africa, this made him conspicuous rather than the reverse. If he had covered the scar by burning his face, he might have been wiser. He also dyed both his hair and his beard black, a fact which one of his neighbors noticed, but attributed to vanity and the quest for the semblance of youth. Placing excessive confidence in his disguise, Fischer had not taken the trouble to study his own telltale mannerisms, such as grasping the corner of his spectacles when talking to people, and systematically to unlearn them.

Fischer spent his time writing a policy article for the *African Communist*, in correspondence with "Kim," the code name for the Overseas Committee, and with women. His major emphases were on the need to recover from the devastating blows which the Security Branch had rained on the underground Party and to tighten security to make the organization invulnerable. An offensive and indomitable spirit and an attitude toward security characteristic of the professional revolutionary were, in his view, the most urgent needs of the hour. In addition, he contacted trusted members of the underground briefly and in a clandestine manner to keep the organization going.

In October, he was indiscreet enough to picnic with his daughter, Ilse, and her husband, a man named Sholto

Cross, who had spent 154 days in solitary confinement. An informant reported to the Security Branch that he had seen Braam Fischer.

He met with other comrades to read a fundamental paper on the new tasks of the Communist movement. The stress was again on tight security, but also on the need to revive and penetrate mass organizations. "We cannot expect any radical change in South Africa's policy of racial oppression until its economic weakness is exposed and its foundations begin to crack," he asserted. "Mass political action directed toward this end should therefore be the prime object." As the Communists and student sympathizers left the meeting and hurriedly vanished into the night, they were observed by a voluptuous young woman and her escort who were parked in a red convertible. Both were police agents.

After considerable hesitation, Braam took the risk of writing an appeal to the Reverend Beyers Naudé, an Afrikaner theologian and a leading light in the liberal-to-progressive Christian Institute. Fischer appealed for cooperation between them to save true Afrikaner culture, and referred to Christ's philosophy, the brotherhood of man and the plight of the non-Whites. Communism, class struggle and the necessity for armed insurrection were played down. Unfortunately for Braam, the police considered the Christian Institute sufficiently suspect to tap its files and photograph or remove their contents. Fischer's letter proved to the authorities that Braam was in the Johannesburg area. Interestingly enough, the original was removed from the files by unknown hands, but apparently not with sufficient promptness.

Braam Fischer was deeply impressed with the extreme measures of security resorted to by the Portuguese Communist Party and particularly by the underground Red activities in support of FRELIMO, the Mozambique terrorist organization, led by Dr. Eduardo Mondlane and by his corps of subversives trained in Red China, Algeria and the Soviet Union. One of the more interesting documents penned by Fischer during his last weeks of freedom was entitled "Notes on the Experiences of our Portuguese Branch." This and similar documents and directives revealed his constant and legitimate obsession with security. Some of the rules he imposed are worth quoting *in extenso*:

. . . No person can take part in underground activity unless he has broken all connection with family and friends. Where it is possible, facilities are made available for correspondence, but his family must never know where he is, or his new identity.

They even insist that those who are unknown to the police and who form part of the underground leadership must change their identity. Their special experience has taught them that the demands of this form of activity require a complete break with normal life.[22]

The underground operator must make only limited use of public transport, leave his residence as seldom as possible, and never re-enter the residence unless he sees a pre-arranged safety signal displayed.

Meetings are as short as possible. The ideal being two or three minutes. There is always an alternative time and place in case the original fails to meet required standards. . . . If any comrade is arrested, every activity with which he was connected is immediately suspended until there is certainty as to his behavior. . . .[23]

On November 9, 1965, the police arrested Mrs. Violet Weinberg, a veteran Communist. She was one of the many

[22]"They" refers to the Portuguese Communist leadership.
[23]Vermaak, *op. cit.*, pp. 219–220.

women who had visited Braam and a key to his house was found in her handbag. By tracing the movements of Fischer's women, the police were able to round up such key members of the tattered and broken Communist apparatus as Ivan Schermbrucker, a member of the Central Committee. The so-called D Group, mainly composed of students and youth about which Ludi had heard reports, was detected and destroyed because of Fischer's decision to skip bail rather than stand trial with his comrades.

Fischer was arrested in November 1965 and put on trial a few months later. This time the charge was sabotage which could carry the death penalty. Specifically, Fischer was accused of having conspired "to further recruitment of persons for instruction and training in the preparation, manufacture and use of explosives to commit acts of violence and destruction in South Africa" and of having trained and instructed these people "in the art of warfare, including guerrilla warfare and military training generally, for the purpose of causing a violent revolution in the Republic."

He was also charged with conspiring to bomb Government buildings and installations and to commit arson by burning the houses of Government officials. Finally, he was accused of writing and publishing Communist articles and directives "to establish in South Africa a despotic system of government based on the dictatorship of the proletariat. . . ."

When Hlapane, one of the Bantu co-opted to the Central Committee of the Party, had been released from 90-day detention, he had assured the comrades that he had behaved "very bravely" and had revealed nothing. At Braam Fischer's trial, this same Hlapane appeared as the star witness of the Government. He testified that Braam

Fischer had personally advocated arson as a political weapon and that, when Joe Slovo had needed money to finance the sabotage and terrorist operations of *Umkhonto We Sizwe,* he had had to go to Braam Fischer to get it.

On March 23, 1966, Fischer was sentenced to life imprisonment. When I was in Pretoria in the fall of that year, I was told that Fischer had to spend days of unrelieved monotony sewing burlap bags in Pretoria prison. It was a terrible end for a man whose youth had been so promising that some of his elders had believed that he was destined to be either Chief Justice of South Africa or its Prime Minister. The deprivation of mental and emotional stimulus of prison life is far more intolerable for men of intelligence and creativity than for the mediocre or subnormal. Consequently, a marked psychological deterioration had already changed Braam Fischer's personality and intelligence for the worse. While they regarded him as the man who had been their most dangerous and worthy enemy, the South African National Police were concerned about this disintegration and were exploring the possibility of changing the conditions of Braam Fischer's confinement.

✧ ✧ ✧ ✧ ✧

CHAPTER ELEVEN

The Battle for Rhodesia

"In previous chapters I attempted to put in this classification a new type of man who today predominates in the world: I called him the mass-man, and I observed that his main characteristic lies in that, feeling himself 'common,' he proclaims the right to be common, and refuses to accept any order superior to himself. It was only natural that, if this mentality is predominant in every people, it should be manifest also when we consider the nations as a group. There are then also relatively mass-peoples determined on rebelling against the great creative peoples, the minority of human stocks which have organized history."

—José Ortega y Gasset, *The Revolt of the Masses*

"The spectacle presented by the United Nations is no more than a vain assertion of equality of influence and power which has no relation to the facts. . . . The United Nations in its present form has to cringe to dictatorships and bully the weak. Small states have no right to speak for the whole of mankind. They must accept, and they would accept, a more intimate but lower rank."

—Sir Winston Churchill

White penetration of what is today Rhodesia began with Scottish missionaries in the 1840's, continued with the explorations of Livingstone and Stanley, and became of major political importance when Cecil Rhodes obtained exclusive mineral concessions in the "Matabele Kingdom" and a Charter from Queen Victoria in 1899 authorizing his British South Africa Company to govern the region. The original Native inhabitants of the land, Bushmen and Hottentots, were exterminated by the advancing Bantu. When Rhodes' 200 picked settlers and 500 Company police entered Rhodesia, the warrior Matabele nation was engaged in practicing genocide against its fellow Bantu nation, the Mashona, whose members they referred to as "dogs." These two tribes successively fought each other and turned on the small White communities, shooting, spearing and clubbing to death men, women and children. Toward the turn of the century, Rhodes and his forces subdued both, established order in the land and brought about a cessation of tribal warfare.

Southern Rhodesia (the Rhodesia of today) attracted White settlement of a sort superior to that which populated most other portions of the British Empire.[1] As popu-

---

[1] In contrast with the Dominions, "the emigration to Rhodesia has been class-selective, the settlers being drawn primarily from the upper and middle classes. The fundamental reason for this was a colonial policy which sought to prevent the settlement of East Africa by indigent Whites on the theory that this would exacerbate the race problem. Unskilled, uneducated, incompetent and unemployable elements were consistently excluded." This is very different from the Australian and New Zealand experience where convicts and unskilled laborers contributed significantly to White settlement. The recent influx of White refugees from Kenya, Uganda, the Congo, and other African areas that experienced Black rule has reinforced the class character of Rhodesian White settlement. Finally, White Rhodesia has a heavy Scottish component and Scots test higher on intelligence tests than Englishmen.

When I was in Rhodesia in November 1966, the Honorable Arthur Philip Smith, Minister of Education, made mental-test scores available to me, based on the South African Group Intelligence Test and for those scoring 130+ on the Terman-Merrill. Proportionately from two to three times as many White Rhodesian public school children as White American, British or New Zealand school children scored above 130, and the Rhodesian contribution at the I.Q. level of 160 and above was even more markedly superior. v. Nathaniel Weyl, "The Intelligence of White Rhodesians," *Intelligence, The Mensa Journal*, No. 97, March 1967, p. 1.

lation grew, government by company charter became obviously unsatisfactory. In 1922 at Winston Churchill's suggestion, the Rhodesian electorate was permitted to choose between incorporation in South Africa and self-government. The electorate chose the latter and from 1923 to the present the country has been self-governing.

In 1953, a Federation of Northern and Southern Rhodesia and Nyasaland was created. The advanced and progressive state of Southern Rhodesia welcomed the union on the theory that: "It is up to us to save Central Africa by our exertions and Africa by our example."[2]

During the decade that followed, Whitehall was under the unrelenting pressure of Black African nationalists and terrorists; the Congo was about to be convulsed in civil war and anarchy; the belief that White colonialism had been an evil thing and that the "winds of change" blowing in the non-White world required a total abdication of European sovereignty in Africa had become part of the creed of the British Establishment.

Toward the close of 1961, Sir Roy Welensky, the Prime Minister of Southern Rhodesia, was naive enough to remind Sir Harold Macmillan of the unequivocal pledges the British Government had given not even to consider the Black nationalist demands to disrupt the Federation. The British Prime Minister's reply was characteristically evasive and Sir Roy later recalled feeling himself smothered "by clouds of chilly cotton wool." Welensky was then brought before other high British officials and "a huge array of African nationalists" and was obliged to listen to "many hours of their oratory with all its prejudice, racial hatred,

[2]The quotation is from the then Prime Minister of Southern Rhodesia, Sir Godfrey Huggins. For a succinct account of the political background, v. Douglas Reed, *The Battle for Rhodesia.* Cape Town: Haum, 1966, pp. 17–39.

special pleading and demand for immediate and total political power."[3] When Sir Roy asked whether the British Government intended to destroy the Federation, he was wished a happy Christmas and a pleasant journey home.

The first Black republic to be carved out of the Federation was impoverished Nyasaland (now rechristened Malawi). By early 1963, Northern Rhodesia became independent as the republic of Zambia with Kenneth Kaunda its president-dictator. The Commonwealth Secretary of the Conservative Government, Duncan Sandys, explained Whitehall's headlong retreat from its commitments in Africa on the grounds that "we British have lost the will to govern." This harassed official was the son-in-law of Winston Churchill!

The great prize in the dominion, which Rhodes had carved out for a more virile British generation, was not Zambia or Malawi, but Rhodesia. With its large and energetic White minority, its modern cities and mines, thriving export agriculture and modern hydroelectric power, Rhodesia enjoyed the highest standards of income, education and health of any African nation south of the Sahara, the Republic of South Africa excepted. Seizure of this prize involved the creation of combat organizations, the training of cadres and the spreading of terror through the Black population until the power of the tribal Chiefs, the rule of tribal law and the acceptance of traditional norms of behavior would be destroyed, as the Mau Mau had sought to destroy these institutional patterns in Kenya. The success of this venture required that the British Government, with its obsessive belief that instant democracy could be imposed upon Black Africa, do everything within its power to thwart White efforts at self-defense, to de-

[3]Reed, *op. cit.*, p. 33, quoting Welensky.

stroy tribal authority and to hail the largely self-appointed
leaders of the nationalist and terrorist bands as the authen-
tic voices of "modern Africa."

Beginnings of an African Communist Network

Uncoordinated Soviet and Communist efforts to sub-
vert tropical African colonies date from before World
War II. A pioneer was George Padmore, a Howard Uni-
versity graduate and for many years the leading Negro
Communist in the British Empire. Padmore indoctrinated
Kwame Nkrumah in Marxism-Leninism and thus gave
the Soviet Union a base in Ghana during the years
Nkrumah ruled there.[4]

At the diagonally opposite end of sub–Saharan Africa,
a hard-core Communist element touched off the Madagascar rebellion of 1947, in which tribal warriors went
into battle protected by amulets of hollowed-out crocodile
teeth, stuffed with spit and excrement. The uprising
changed into a race war, saturated with fetishism, in
which the insurgents destroyed 8,500 plantations and murdered countless Malagasy who had betrayed tribalism by
seeking cultural and civic assimilation with the French.
In this three-year struggle, at least 80,000 people lost their
lives, many by slow and cruel tortures.[5]

A coordinated Kremlin effort to subvert Africa south
of the Sahara dates from the Bandung Conference of
African and Asian Peoples of 1955. In May 1956, the
Central Committee of the Communist Party of the Soviet

[4]The son of a Trinidad physician, his real name was Cream. Padmore
was his Party *nom de guerre*. He objected to the popular front policy
and fell from Kremlin grace in 1935. v. George S. Schuyler, *Black and
Conservative*. New Rochelle: Arlington House, 1966, p. 146.
[5]Arthur Stratton, *The Great Red Island*. London: Macmillan, 1965,
p. 246.

Union directed that the activities of all international Red front organizations be coordinated in the Academy of Science of the U.S.S.R., and shortly thereafter, a lower echelon coordinating agency, the Afro-Asian Peoples' Solidarity Organization (AAPSO), was set up in Cairo.[6]

Chinese efforts in this area began at about the same time, but developed more slowly. Mao's men believed that, as non-Whites, they would get a more favorable reception among the African Natives than the Russians. The lack of industrial development and the general technological backwardness of the area made the example of China's successive revolutions and her long period of partisan war in the countryside more relevant than the October Revolution in Soviet Russia. The Chinese tended to concentrate on using the most leftist elements in the Black states to overthrow the existing regimes and move the revolutionary struggle forward, whereas the Soviets have more frequently worked with the Black governments. The Chinese concentration area has tended to be East Africa and the Congo, jeopardizing Soviet designs on the Indian Ocean area. Here, the disintegration of British power in the Indian Ocean and the increasing prestige and influence of the Soviet Union in Moslem countries after the six-day war have aided and accelerated Russian penetration. While the long-range objectives of the two great Communist powers were in conflict and perhaps mutually incompatible, there was a considerable degree of cooperation in practical operations until the Third Council Meeting of AAPSO at Bandung, at which evidence of Sino-Soviet conflict within the organization became overwhelming. Even subsequent to this meeting, however, guerrillas trained in

[6]Alejandro Botzaris, *Communist Penetration in Africa.* Lisbon, 1961, pp. 52–53, 1–10.

Communist China would often cooperate in operations against Rhodesia, Angola and Mozambique with others trained in Soviet and Soviet-satellite areas.

In 1964, shortly after Chou En-lai had proclaimed that Africa would be "the next storm center of the world revolution," an uprising broke out in Zanzibar in which some 2,000 Arabs were slaughtered and potential opponents were buried alive.[7] The one-party dictatorship that emerged turned the island into a Chinese Communist satellite. Although the revolution had been engineered in part by the Chinese Communist agent Mohammed Babu, the United States and Britain promptly recognized the new regime.[8]

At about the same time, Chinese agents touched off an attempted revolution and civil war in the eastern Congo. Writing in *Figaro* on December 10–12, 1964, Max Clos commented on the fact that the Chinese Reds encourage fetishism, previously regarded in Africa as "a hidden, almost shameful thing." Reasoning that the Congolese natives were incapable of any political or ideological indoctrination, the Chinese used fetishism to "liberate" the Natives from European civilization and, for this reason, concentrated on the slaughter of priests and missionaries.

"The second specialized field in which Chinese Communists are intensifying their efforts," Clos continued, "is that represented by the setting up and empowering of people's tribunals; their task is to condemn to death and carry out public executions of those convicted."[9] One pur-

---

[7]Cyrus L. Sulzberger in the *New York Times*, August 4, 1964.

[8]The *New York Herald Tribune* observed editorially: "Today any mob, any agitator who wins power can expropriate property, arrest aliens at will, or indulge in outright murder . . . and if this is done in the sacred name of nationalism and popular will, there is no redress."

[9]Quoted in Rev. Paul Crane, S.J., *Red China in Africa*. New York: American–African Affairs Association, undated, pp. 12–13.

pose was to involve the masses in the revolution and to make them guilty accomplices. Another apparent purpose was to exterminate those elements in the Native population that had been touched by Western civilization so as to enable the Chinese Communists to start again from scratch. An observer who was in the Congo during the Chinese-inspired Simba troubles told me that the criterion of whether a Native was to be allowed to live or to be killed was whether he wore shoes.

Meanwhile, the struggle for control of AAPSO, and hence of the Marxist-Leninist revolutionary movement in the underdeveloped world, was coming to a head. On March 23, 1963, Mrs. Kuo Chien, the leader of the Chinese delegation to the Sixth Council Meeting of AAPSO in Algiers, accused the Soviet Union of having betrayed the Congo and of moral guilt for the murder of Patrice Lumumba. She also assailed Khrushchev's advocacy of peaceful coexistence and the nuclear test ban.[10]

Nevertheless, between 1963 and 1967, the U.S.S.R. gained complete control over AAPSO. Its political resolutions consistently reflected Moscow's ideology and consistently justified whatever action the Kremlin took. Because of the unreliability of the Castro regime from the Soviet standpoint, Latin America was excluded from AAPSO and the Havana Afro-Asian Latin American Peoples' Solidarity Organization (AALAPSO) remained largely an empty shell. The East European Soviet client states were allowed to send fraternal delegations to AAPSO meetings, although none was an Asian or African power. Control over AAPSO was vested in the Cairo Secretariat

[10]International Documentation and Information Centre, *Afro-Asian Peoples' Solidarity Organization* (AAPSO) The Hague, February 1969, pp. 34–38.

under Yussef el Sebai, an Egyptian Communist and an obedient follower of the Kremlin line. Finally, wherever two Communist or Communist-infiltrated political movements competed for leadership, AAPSO recognized the one subordinate to the Kremlin and excluded the one loyal to Peking. In South West Africa, the pro-Chinese SWANU delegation was denied admission and the pro-Kremlin South West African People's Organization (SWAPO) was accredited. The Pan Africanist Congress (PAC) in South Africa and the National Zimbabwe Union (ZANU) were denied admittance as were Peking-dominated Japanese and Ceylonese Communist groups. On November 6, 1967, the Permanent Secretariat of AAPSO rejected the pro-Chinese Mozambique terrorist organization, COREMO. In August 1968, in Cairo, the Secretariat gave exclusive accreditation to the African National Congress (ANC) in South Africa, ZAPU in Rhodesia, MPLA in Angola, and the FRELIMO movement in Mozambique.[11]

Terror in Rhodesia

After negotiation with African Nationalists, Asians, Coloured and the opposition National Democratic Party, Rhodesia promulgated a new Constitution in 1961, which was approved by the electorate. Unlike South Africa, the franchise in Rhodesia was not based upon race, but upon property and education. The qualifications for the "A" roll, which elected a majority of the seats in Parliament, were income of £792 or property worth £1,650 for those with no schooling, but income of merely £330 per annum or property worth £550 for those with four years of sec-

[11]*Ibid.*, pp. 54–59.

ondary schooling. Under the "B" roll, which elected 15 seats, the qualifications were even lower. At the close of 1966, it was estimated that 95,700 Whites and 2,400 Blacks voted on the "A" roll and 10,780 Blacks and 589 Whites on the "B" roll. However, about 60,000 Africans were believed qualified by education and property for the "A" roll and only apathy toward politics prevented them from voting.[12] Since vast efforts were being made to expand Native education as rapidly as possible, since Rhodesian cash income for all racial groups was increasing steadily until the boycott and since the world is in an inflationary era, it was evident that the Constitution would have provided for a Black majority in a fairly brief period of time.[13] Thus, it appears that the purpose of the Black nationalist leaders in resorting to boycott of the referendum on the Constitution and a campaign of terrorism was to obtain power through revolutionary means, and therefore total power.

Since Rhodesia has been damned in the Western press as a racist society, it is perhaps worth adding that the University College of Rhodesia in Salisbury is not only multiracial, but offers scholarships to non-White students who would not qualify if of European descent. Hotels, bars, restaurants and other public places are not racially segregated by law, though they may be so by custom and preference. One out of six Africans attends school in Rhodesia as compared with one in 18 in Tanzania, one in 40 in Liberia and one in 108 in Ethiopia. African education is the largest item in the Rhodesian budget and

[12]James Jackson Kilpatrick, Réné Albert Wormser and Walter Darnell Jacobs, "Rhodesia: a Case History," *National Review*, May 16, 1967, p. 517.
[13]Of course, as Black majority rule impended, the electorate might have revised the Constitution to prevent it.

normally accounts for about 9 per cent of total outlay. Advancement in the civil service is based on competition, not race, and the large majority of the armed forces of Rhodesia consist of Africans.

Having earlier decided to support the new Constitution, the National Democratic Party withdrew support in late 1960 and the campaign of violence started. The scale of the operation is indicated by the fact that, during the two-month period August–September 1962, 15 schools and 8 churches were burned down, 25 gasoline bomb attacks took place and 11 Africans were assaulted. The violence was directed almost exclusively against Africans who cooperated with the authorities.

These acts of violence were generally directed by Blacks who had been infiltrated over the border and sent to Lusaka in Zambia for further assignment by the terrorist headquarters there. Proceeding via Dar es Salaam, they would be moved to training centers abroad for basic military training. Those with leadership or technical potential might be sent to the Soviet Union, Red China, Czechoslovakia or Eastern Germany.

During the two-year period that followed the breakup of the Federation, the terror campaign against the tribal Chiefs continued and the latter clamored for governmental protection. In the summer of 1964, Rhodesian Prime Minister Ian Smith sent 29 senior Chiefs to visit Europe. The British Prime Minister refused to see them, but Duncan Sandys told them that the terrorist leaders, whom he called "African nationalists," had the support of the people. The Chiefs retorted that any following they had was obtained by intimidation and murder, whereupon Sandys replied that he was not interested in their methods. The tribal Chiefs replied that, in that case, they would send out their *impis* (Zulu for "band of Native warriors") and wipe the terrorists off the face of the earth, but Sandys expressed horror and disapproval of such violence.[14]

During seven weeks of that summer, 1,725 acts of terrorism occurred, including murder. The Rhodesian Government, which had banned the National Democratic Party in December 1961, now outlawed its successor ZAPU (Zimbabwe African People's Union) and ZANU (Zimbabwe African National Union), a splinter group of ZAPU. Reverend Dr. Ndabaningi Sithole, the Maoist Communist and formidable leader of ZANU, was collared and jailed under emergency legislation. At this writing, Dr. Sithole remains in prison, which seems an appropriate place for a person of that name. After the vigorous security measures of 1964–65, the wave of terrorism at least temporarily subsided.

In 1965, the Labour Party was swept into power and a politician named Arthur Bottomley became Colonial Secretary. Bottomley, who was so ignorant of Africa that he once confused Zambia with Gambia, was sent to Rhodesia to negotiate. "He was," Reed writes, "a natural master of the *mot injuste* and aroused in others the unease which the sight of a hippopotamus walking on eggs would cause."[15]

Since the Chiefs had not proceeded in accordance with British parliamentary procedure, Bottomley concluded that they had not resorted to democratic procedures and were trying to deceive him. In fact, they had held an *Indaba*, or council meeting, at which over 600 Chiefs from all over Rhodesia had discussed independence from Britain for five days and had concluded that the protection

[14]Reed, *op. cit.*, p. 49.
[15]*Ibid.*, pp. 51–52.

of the Great Britain of the 1960's was not worth having. As is customary, they had not voted, but had discussed until they reached a consensus. "I am astounded to hear that the Chiefs and Headmen are not the leaders of the people," a tribal Chief told Bottomley.

What have you been doing for seventy years that you have not discovered this before?

Many of the Chiefs and Headmen here present have had their wives and children killed. . . . Everywhere the people are fighting like dogs over a bone because power was let fall into wrong hands. . . . We live in fear because the Europeans overseas are giving our youngsters bombs and weapons. . . . When we went to London, the British Ministers ran away and hid. One of them said, "I can see you for thirty minutes" and then had the nerve to tell us, "You are not the leaders of the people, Nkomo is the leader. . . ."[16]

I stand so that you can see me, your servant who has had his houses burned and children and wives killed.

Rhodes set us our great example when he said that everybody must work together, put down their weapons and work as one community, and we did this and have lived very happily together. Had we known that this would be changed, we certainly would not have laid aside our weapons.

From the time when I was a child, brought up by my fathers, the old people, they always made me understand that the British word and the British sense of justice was something that one had to look up to. . . . Now we have doubts whether England is still England . . . and we are left with the impression that those who hold the reins in England are no longer British, probably some other nationality.[17]

Having learned little or nothing from his meeting with the Chiefs at Domboshawa in March 1965, Bottomley returned to London and reported to Prime Minister Wil-

[16]Joshua Nkomo was the leader of the National Democratic Party, the terrorist organization outlawed in 1961.
[17]Reed, *op. cit.*, pp. 52–53.

son. The latter made the extraordinary statement that the Chiefs could not "by the wildest stretch of the imagination" be considered to represent the African people. The facts of the matter were that the Chiefs represented the tribally organized Bantu, comprising a preponderance of Rhodesia's 4,000,000 Blacks, whereas the strength of the terrorists was confined primarily to the urban centers, to detribalized Africans and to immigrant workers from other Black states.

The response of Rhodesia to the breakdown of negotiations with Britain was to issue a Unilateral Declaration of Independence (UDI) on November 11, 1965. At Britain's request, the United Nations condemned this action the following day and urged member states not to assist the Ian Smith regime. On November 20, the U.N. imposed voluntary sanctions on Rhodesia.

These sanctions were of limited efficacy. The tobacco industry was hard hit. Since tobacco is an intensive-labor crop, closure of export markets for Rhodesian leaf meant hardship and unemployment for African farm workers. Adequate supplies of petroleum were brought in from South Africa and the shortage of import goods stimulated the creation of new Rhodesian industries for the home market.

On December 16, 1966, the United Nations branded Rhodesia "a threat to international peace." President Johnson's Ambassador to the United Nations, Arthur Goldberg, immediately pledged United States support for sanctions against Rhodesia "in order to drive home to the illegal regime [of Ian Smith] that the international community will not tolerate the existence of a discriminatory system based on minority rule in defiance of the United Nations and its principles."

Ambassador Goldberg's logic was extraordinary, to say the least. Over half of the 122 U.N. member states had governments not based upon majority rule. The "illegality" of the regime should not have impressed any American familiar with the history of his own country. As for the United Nations statement that Rhodesia threatened international peace, the statement simply reversed the facts of the matter. Rhodesia was exposed to attacks by guerrillas, armed, financed, trained and abetted by Black African member states of the United Nations in flagrant defiance of the U.N. Charter. She had no aggressive aims against any of these states, since the Rhodesian White minority is intelligent enough to prosper during peacetime, since it has no desire to acquire tropical rural slums and since any conquests would make the 225,000 White citizens of the country an even smaller minority than they already were. However, Ambassador Goldberg had shown on previous occasions that, where racial issues were involved, he practiced a double standard of morality in favor of Black demands.

"Whatever the Rhodesians have done," Dean Acheson, former Secretary of State under President Truman, observed in a letter to the *Washington Post*,[18] "has been wholly within their own country and contains no element of aggression." Acheson added that, since its Charter "provides unequivocally that the United Nations shall not intervene within the internal jurisdiction of any state," its action against Rhodesia was illegal.

Senator Harry F. Byrd, Jr., of Virginia asked why the United States should help Britain regain a colony, which had followed in America's footsteps by declaring her independence, at a time when British ships were delivering

[18]December 31, 1966.

matériel of war to our Vietcong enemy. Representative H. R. Gross of Iowa went further and asked: "When, if ever, will the fatheads in this Administration come to their senses and recognize that to destroy Rhodesia and the prosperity and stability it represents in southern Africa can only serve the interests of the Communists?"[19]

Presidential orders in support of United Nations sanctions made it a crime for American citizens to export to or import from Rhodesia a list of proscribed commodities. Violation of these regulations was made punishable by a fine of up to $10,000 and imprisonment for up to ten years. Thoughtful Americans were deeply concerned about the implications of these measures under which the President could sidestep the Congress and proclaim what actions in violation of U.N. resolutions were crimes and what punishments should attach to them. Speaking before the American Bar Association in the spring of 1968 on the "Arrogance of International Lawyers," Dean Acheson used strong language in characterizing American policy toward Rhodesia: "It will surprise some of our fellow citizens, though hardly anyone here today, to be told that the United States is engaged in an international conspiracy, instigated by Britain and blessed by the United Nations, to overthrow the government of a country that has done us no harm and threatened no one. This is barefaced aggression, unprovoked and unjustified by a single legal or moral principle."

Ambassador Goldberg was not alone in his fanatical hostility to White rule in Africa. Mennen Williams, President Johnson's Assistant Secretary of State for African Affairs, allegedly urged on television "bringing down the

[19]v. "Crackdown on Rhodesia: Another Country for U.S. to 'Rescue'?" *U. S. News & World Report*, January 2, 1967, pp. 28–29.

South African Government."[20] While the maladroit and bumptious Williams was eventually removed from his post, President Johnson himself demanded that "legitimate government" be established in Rhodesia to "open the full power and responsibility of nationhood to all the people of Rhodesia, not just six per cent," adding that "we will not support policies abroad which are based on the rule of minorities or the discredited notion that men are unequal before the law."[21] If this doctrine had been applied seriously and impartially, it would have run counter to Mr. Johnson's vigorous efforts to stimulate American trade with Iron Curtain countries. However, it was not intended that it apply impartially. The exclusive target was those nations settled by White people of European stock, living under institutions of due process of law and engaged in a struggle against Communism for their survival.

Whether by design or inadvertence, these and similar pronouncements by American and British political leaders stimulated Black African chiefs of state to believe they had Anglo-American support in their efforts to overthrow the White governments of Southern Africa. They made the recruitment of terrorists easier and gave the various terrorist organizations national and international prestige, enabling them to raise the funds they needed for their murderous work from "respectable" circles.

The same policies were applied to South Africa with similar effect. Let us consider a few of them. When Andrew Carnegie founded the Carnegie Endowment for International Peace in the hopes of removing the scourge of war from the world's people, he could not have foreseen some of the malign purposes for which his fortune would

[20]According to Reed, *op cit.*, pp. 127–28.
[21]*Ibid.*, p. 129.

subsequently be spent. In the 1940's, the people who ran the Carnegie Foundation were so leftist or so politically naive that they offered its presidency to Alger Hiss, the State Department official who would shortly thereafter be convicted of perjury in connection with his activities as a Soviet spy.

In 1965, this same Carnegie Endowment furthered the cause of world peace by publishing a book-length work entitled *Apartheid and United Nations Collective Measures.* It was distributed to all United Nations representatives in New York, and was authored in part by an anonymous member of the staff of the Military Academy at West Point, and had the blessing, if not much more, of the African Affairs Bureau of the State Department. This 170-page volume contained a blueprint, worked out in detail, for the invasion and conquest of South Africa. Total requirements included 93,000 troops, 145 warships and ancillary craft, 300 combat and 200 transport aircraft, 30 days in the field and an outlay of $95,000,000. This program for an unprovoked assault on a friendly power was generally attributed to the group of leftist politicians around Mennen Williams, Arthur Goldberg, and Robert F. Kennedy. Proposals of this sort for military aggression against South Africa and Rhodesia were consistently opposed by Secretary of State Dean Rusk, a statesmen who never managed to forget that the headquarters of his country's enemies were not in Salisbury and Pretoria, but in Moscow and Peking.

A similar incident was the trip of Senator Robert F. Kennedy to South Africa in 1966. Kennedy spoke before "liberal" student audiences under the sponsorship of the National Union of South African Students (NUSAS). This was a leftist organization in consistent opposition to the Government. Its 1963 president, Adrian Leftwich, had been one of the main leaders of the African Resistance Movement (ARM), which had engaged in dynamiting railroad tracks and electric power pylons. Brought to trial in late 1964, the student revolutionary terrorists received long prison sentences. Leftwich escaped punishment by turning state's evidence, which induced the trial judge to take exception to the fact that the defense counsel for two of the other defendants had called him a rat on the grounds that, "I am not sure that it is not a trifle hard on the genus *rattus*."[22]

Appearing under these distinguished auspices, Senator Kennedy made the usual denunciations of Apartheid. He then proceeded to Uganda, where the gunmen of Dictator Obote were engaged in massacring the Buganda tribe, but this did not inspire him to further moralizing. Arriving at Dar es Salaam, the headquarters of the terrorist murder operations against South Africa, Rhodesia and Portugal's African possessions, Kennedy alleged that there was "a special bond of friendship between the United States and Tanzania" and "a common commitment to work for human justice and equality." Tanzania was and is a leftist dictatorship and its island department, Zanzibar, was controlled by Communist China and had recently been the scene of a massacre of the Arab population accompanied by revolting acts of cruelty.[23] These facts were sufficiently notorious to have occasioned highly critical articles and editorials in the *New York Times* and *New York Herald Tribune*.

The third episode was that of South West Africa.

[22]Miles Brokensha and Robert Knowles, *The Fourth of July Raids*. Cape Town: Simondium Publishers, 1965, p. 144.
[23]Reed, *op. cit.*, pp. 149–51.

Liberia and Ethiopia, serving in this instance as cat's-paws of the State Department, brought charges against South Africa before the International Court, alleging that she had violated the terms of her League of Nations mandate over South West Africa and was oppressing its people. Three days before the verdict, Ambassador Goldberg pledged the United States to see that the decision of the Court was enforced. The International Court declared, much to Goldberg's chagrin, that the charges against South Africa were false or unproven, and sustained the mandate. Ambassador Goldberg then observed that the decision was of "limited scope" and "very unhelpful."

Encouraged by this, the Afro-Asian block induced the U.N. General Assembly to terminate the South African mandate and set up a shadow United Nations Government for South West Africa.[24] South Africa refused to recognize this rump government or to abandon its control of an area vital to its strategic security. In July 1967, U Thant addressed a United Nations seminar on Apartheid in Zambia and recommended that the Black African states assist in the organization of "national liberation movements," a proposal contrary to the avowed policies of the U.N.[25]

Terrorist groups had been discovered operating in South West Africa in August 1966 and March 1967. The matter had been regarded as sufficiently serious to send General van den Bergh to the area to work out effective counter measures. In August 1967, 37 South West African Natives

[24]The United States, Great Britain, the Soviet Union and France abstained from voting for the resolution.
[25]General Assembly Resolution 2131 (XX) of December 21, 1965, declares that "no state shall organize, assist, foment, finance, incite or tolerate subversive, terrorist or armed activities directed to the violent overthrow of the regime of another state."

were tried in Pretoria for such offenses as receiving terrorist training abroad, conspiring to commit murder, raiding a Government outpost and farm, and entering the country with arms to bring about "violent revolution."

The United Nations stridently protested the trial on the theory that South Africa no longer had the right to govern her mandate and U Thant described the prisoners as "South West African leaders." On September 12, the United Nations Committee on Colonialism condemned South Africa for "the illegal arrest of 37 African nationalists" and demanded the prisoners be released forthwith. The Organization of African States simultaneously ordered that staff officers be provided for the "freedom fighter" operations against White Southern Africa.

South Africa refused to be intimidated or to allow the United Nations shadow government to enter its mandated territory. The trial proceeded under emergency legislation of a far-reaching sort. Prime Minister Vorster observed: "Instead of dealing with suspected terrorists by summarily executing them, as is so often the case elsewhere," the accused were being tried fairly and by due process. He added that "it remains our declared intention to fight this form of international gangsterism here and wherever else we are allowed to do so."

On January 26, 1968, 30 of the accused were convicted and sentenced to terms ranging from five years imprisonment to life. Trial Judge Ludorf found that the guilty men had

attacked defenseless citizens, White and non-White, after they had determined by reconnaissance that these citizens were indeed defenseless. Their conduct was not that of "freedom fighters," but the conduct of cowards, assassins and ordinary criminals. . . . In my view, it has been proved that the accused, because of the level of their civilization, became the easy mis-guided dupes of Communist indoctrination. Had it not been for the active financial and practical assistance which the accused received from the governments of Moscow, Peking and other countries, they would never have found themselves in their present predicament. I also think that had it not been for the loud-mouthed moral support and incitement by repre-sentatives of foreign countries . . . the accused would never have embarked on their futile and ill-conceived exploits.

The 1969 Rhodesian Constitution

Probably because of pressures from the powerful liberal group within the Rhodesian Front and from business inter-ests allied to Great Britain, Prime Minister Ian Smith found himself under increasing pressure to urge constitu-tional reform.[26] In March 1967, he appointed the so-called Whaley Commission to frame a new Constitution, which issued somewhat ambiguous recommendations in April 1968 that were approved by a special congress of the Rho-desian Front five months later.

The Rhodesian Government soon became convinced that the Labour Government would not accept the Whaley compromises. Despite the voluble opposition of Bishop Paul Burroughs of Mashonaland and of small, strident groups in the multiracial University College of Salisbury, Smith declared on May 21, 1969, that the "intractable attitude" of Britain made compromise impossible and total independence from the Crown indispensable. On the fol-lowing day, he proposed a new constitutional framework, modelled partly on the Whaley Report, and a national referendum to approve or reject it.

The new national charter provided for total segregation

[26]A. J. van Wyk, "Rhodesia, Constitutional Proposals," *Bulletin of the Afrika Instituut* (January–February 1969), pp. 19–28.

of voter rolls, looking toward eventual equal representation of Whites and Blacks when the latter paid their proportionate share of income taxes. In the first phase of operations, there would be 16 African representatives in a 66-member House, of whom eight would be elected and eight nominees of the tribal Chiefs.

These proposals stirred the *New York Times* to genteel indignation. On May 22, 1969, the *Times* headline read: "Rhodesia Offered a Constitution Perpetuating Control by Whites." In the body of the story, however, the *Times* correspondent conceded that "Africans are offered eventual parity in parliamentary representation. . . ." It had evidently not occurred to the editors of that once magisterial organ that perpetual control by Whites is logically inconsistent with eventual parity for Blacks.

The new Constitution aroused the protests of former Prime Minister Sir Roy Welensky, who regarded it as a repudiation of the ideals Cecil Rhodes had stood for. The Conservative Association and the Candour League attacked the new proposals as designed to "entrench multiracialism," lead to chaos and open up the specter of a victorious coalition of White liberals and Black Power advocates that could push Rhodesia into the abyss. The *Times* deprecated the fact that people imprisoned under Rhodesia's anti-subversion and anti-terrorism laws would not be eligible for election to the new House until five years after their release from prison. It particularly deplored that the Reverend Ndabaningi Sithole, a Chinese Communist agent whom the *New York Times* characterized as an "African nationalist leader," would not be able to grace the new Rhodesian Parliament with his presence.

On June 20, 1969, the Rhodesian electorate approved the new Constitution by a three-to-one majority and total independence from the British Crown by an even larger vote. To an observer who has sat through two sessions of the Rhodesian Parliament, carefully observed the conduct of its two Negro members and discussed politics with these gentlemen in the tea room of the House, the prospect of an eightfold increase in Black representation does not seem likely to enhance the intellectual caliber of Rhodesian democracy. On the other hand, the fact that half of the Black representatives are to be chosen by the tribal Chiefs seems a reasonable guarantee against the dire forbodings of the Candour League. One is inclined to feel that constitutions are too important to be shaped and transformed to meet temporary political emergencies, but that this one will not materially change the political landscape of Rhodesia.

❖ ❖ ❖ ❖ ❖

CHAPTER TWELVE

The Ring of Terror

"Everyone belongs to all, and all to everyone. All are slaves and equal in their slavery. In extreme cases, there are slander and murder, but the chief thing is equality. To begin with, the level of education, science, and talents is lowered. A high level of science and talents is suitable only for great intellects, and great intellects are not wanted. . . . Slaves are bound to be equal. Without despotism there has never been freedom or equality; but within the herd, there is bound to be despotism."

—FEODOR DOSTOEVSKI, *The Possessed*[1]

THE ARREST OF BRAAM FISCHER AND HIS FELLOW CONSPIRA-tors marked the virtual destruction of the illegal Communist Party organization in South Africa as an effective political force. It can be assumed that a new Red underground has been created, but there is no evidence that it wields power.

After Rivonia, the battle against South Africa began to change in emphasis and direction. In the early 1960's, the strategy had been to rely on a combined operation of the internal forces of subversion and guerrilla fighters and ter-

[1]Speech of Pyotr Verhovensky. Translated by Robert Payne in *Zero: the Story of Terrorism*. New York: John Day, 1950, p. 47.

rorists trained abroad and infiltrated into the target area. After 1965, the Soviets, the Chinese Communists and the more intransigent Black African states began to concentrate almost exclusively on the infiltration of terrorist bands. As in the Arab paramilitary campaign against Israel after the six-day war, the strategic plan was to advance from isolated terrorist operations to full-fledged partisan warfare and to move from partisan warfare to outright, full-scale invasion. In accordance with the doctrines of Mao Tse-tung and Ché Guevara, the timetable of these qualitative leaps from one phase of conflict to the next higher phase cannot be programmed in advance, but depends on the success and tempo of the revolutionary struggle.

Guerrilla forces and terrorists were not deployed against South Africa itself because of difficulty of access and because of the virtual certainty that they would be totally destroyed. The blows were directed rather against the three buffer areas on South Africa's northern and western perimeter: the mandated territory of South West Africa, Rhodesia and Portuguese Mozambique.

The scale of these operations increased until 1968. According to S. L. Muller, South Africa's Deputy Minister of Police, about 900 Bantu were promised "scholarships" for further study abroad between 1963 and 1967; were sent to Dar es Salaam, where they were informed for the first time that they were to receive military training for guerrilla operations, and then were sent to training camps in Egypt, Ghana, Algeria, Russia, Cuba, Red China and North Korea. These men were threatened with physical violence if they refused training. They were unable to escape from the camps because they lacked money or travel documents.

Scope of Military Operations

The Black republics of Tanzania, Zambia and the Congo (Kinshasha) face White Africa on the line of the Zambesi. Between that river and the Zambesi Escarpment some 60 miles to the south, there is a no-man's-land of about 120,000 square miles of bush, *karoo* and jungle, through which infiltration teams are deployed and over which a running, intermittent military conflict smolders. As of September 1968, according to the most reliable and authoritative study available in English of these operations,[2] between 38,000 and 42,000 fully trained *guerrilleros*, situated in 23 camps in Zambia and 13 more in Tanzania, constituted the striking force of the aggressors. In addition, some 28,000 men were in training camps in Algeria, Ethiopia, the Soviet Union, Red China and Cuba. With a basic training course of eight to ten months, some 2,500 fully trained fighters flowed out of the pipeline monthly, were sent to the camps, were armed and were infiltrated across the border with orders to shoot to kill and at all costs to avoid capture.

As against this buildup of invasion forces, there are the losses sustained by death in combat, capture and desertion. Both the Rhodesian and the Portuguese authorities consider this information classified for self-evident security reasons. According to one neutral intelligence estimate,

[2]Daniel T. Brigham, *Blueprint for Conflict*. New York: American–African Affairs Association, 1969, 34 pp. Colonel Brigham, who headed the European Service of the *New York Times* during World War II and was military and foreign affairs editor of the *New York Journal American* from 1950 to 1966, made a six-week intensive survey of the partisan warfare area, comprising Mozambique, Malawi, Rhodesia, Botswana and South West Africa, in September–October 1968. His report, based on 18 hours of taped interviews, including interrogation of 181 terrorists, is an indispensable source upon which I have leaned heavily.

the Portuguese alone were holding 20,000 prisoners in 1968, and another equally authoritative source believed that total guerrilla losses during the four years to mid-1968 were in the neighborhood of 42,000 men.

The strategic plan is divided into three phases. The first, calling for the creation of strong guerrilla striking forces to provide leadership at the noncom and higher levels of a so-called citizen army, is nearing completion. Although the target for the "citizen army" is 100,000 men, there were only about 35,000 irregulars in training in Zambia at the time of the Brigham study.

The second phase is to move enough Soviet and Chinese Communist troops and military technicians to control and dominate the border area along the Zambesi. According to some reports, the Chinese had installed from 50,000 to 75,000 "technicians" on the island of Zanzibar, which they completely control, by mid-1968. They had about 16,000 so-called laborers building a railroad for the Zambian Government to link Lusaka with the port of Dar es Salaam. According to captured terrorists, the Chinese had supplied Zambia with jet fighter planes that had Chinese pilots and remained under Chinese control.

Soviet technicians, military experts, troops and intelligence people were considerably less numerous in East Africa than the Chinese, but the Soviet presence in the Congo—and particularly in Katanga Province, which borders on Zambia—was massive.

The third phase of the operation is supposed to be the invasion of White Africa, the overthrow of its governments and their replacement by Communist or popular-front-type regimes.

As for the terrorists, Brigham concluded that "a minimum of three out of ten recruits for this rebel army have been shanghaied or press-ganged into service by teams roaming on both sides of the front lines. These victims report unspeakable atrocities, employed to ensure their loyalty, in training camps ringed night and day by armed guards."[3]

The teams were commanded by specially trained "commissars" who were supposed to constitute the local military government of the zones in which they fought once the invasion triumphed. A frequent objective of the raids was to murder Rhodesian or Mozambique citizens, generally Negro, who were believed to have informed to the police. This suggested that the terrorists had an intelligence net in both countries.

In the summer of 1968, the South African Broadcasting Corporation put three terrorists, who had been captured by Rhodesian security forces, on the air. These men had been trained in the Soviet Union for periods up to one year. Despite this considerable investment, they were sent without any preliminary planning across the Zambesi at night with general orders to engage the Rhodesian police. One stated that he had been three and a half days without food when he was captured. Although they had been told that the Black population would welcome them with open arms, the one who made contact with the Bantu was promptly betrayed to the authorities. He said that he believed that 48 of the men who had crossed the river with him had been killed and many more captured and that the terrorist forces had no chance of success.

Another of the captured terrorists described the low morale in the camps as due to a realization that they were "just the tools of the leaders or of the Communists." As for conditions in the Zambia camps, he said: "People there

[3]Brigham, *op. cit.*, p. 5.

are suffering from hunger, they have no clothing, no doctors to attend this people. The leaders, they don't care
of these people, they are going with their own beautiful
cars, going to hotel and to some other places with them
is some young girls, yes, they don't attend these people."[4]
He added that when ZAPU and ZANU people met, "they
are fighting among themselves."[5]

Brigham quotes a captured terrorist as telling him that
"things were always better here (in Rhodesia) than they
were over there (in the training camps)."[6]

In addition to hunger and bad conditions, the terrorist
inmates of the camps lived in fear. The captured infiltrators almost invariably "tell of ghoulish tortures and death
meted out to traitors." The Reds carefully select men from
each camp with a special gift for reporting and description
to witness these executions, which generally occur just before the main meal "so that returning witnesses by their
behavior and nausea will achieve added credibility in their
descriptions of the scene." Brigham adds:

The methods include short drops at hangings, so the man-
acled prisoner (usually minus the mercy of a blindfold or
hood) slowly strangles in a dance of death; firing squads that
require three and four *coups de grace* to dispatch the prisoner
while he shrieks for mercy; and scientific beatings to daze the
bound prisoner just long enough for a gasoline fire to burn
deep into his flesh before he recovers to scream in pain until
he dies. There are other, even more vicious, methods and
techniques, but these are enough to give the picture.[7]

[4]"Three Terrorists Speak," *Bulletin of the Afrika Instituut*, Pretoria, Vol.
VI, No. 7 (August 1968), pp. 205–15.
[5]ZAPU and ZANU are the two rival terrorist political organizations seeking to conquer Rhodesia.
[6]Brigham, *op. cit.*, p. 8.
[7]*Ibid.*, p. 21. Brigham adds that a frequent witness of these killings,
although captured months after they had occurred, vomited in the interrogation room when he was questioned about them.

The terrorists are described as better educated than the average African, almost all bilingual and about half of them literate. About 20 per cent are believed to be *bona fide* volunteers, sophisticated enough to understand something of the Communist message. Perhaps 45 per cent are fugitives from justice who fled to the Black republics to escape prosecution for felony. Of the remainder, about half were tricked into recruitment in the belief that they were getting an education. The rest consist of people with grudges against individual White men or White communities and a small group of hippies and curiosity seekers.[8]

These men may be badly fed and wretchedly treated, but they are well armed, the standard weapon being the Russian-designed and Chinese-manufactured AK-47 automatic rifle. In addition, they are supplied with such weapons as hand grenades, anti-tank rocket launchers of the bazooka type, land mines, TNT and plastic explosives. The grenades and mines are generally detonated on impact and charged with TNT.

Counter-Insurgency

Lieutenant General van den Bergh, the advisor to the South African Prime Minister on security matters, told Colonel Brigham that terrorist bands will generally surrender if they believe they are being tracked by White men, but not if their pursuers are Blacks. One reason for this is that loyal Africans have been in the habit of ambushing infiltrators and then slowly beating them to death, leaving one of them sufficiently alive to crawl back to his comrades and report what happened. The Rhodesian, South African and Portuguese authorities do whatever they can to prevent these murders of prisoners.

[8]*Ibid.*, p. 20.

Thirst, fatigue, hunger and fear in that order are the factors most likely to break an infiltrator's will to fight and to induce him to surrender under bush conditions, according to van den Bergh. The security advisor told Brigham that the terrorists trained in Red China held out longest under questioning, that those trained in the Soviet Union were more poised and arrogant when captured and that the Cuban terrorists were the most strongly motivated element and the group most likely to die fighting rather than surrender. The men who received military education in Algeria or Ethiopia had the practical advantage of combat training in desert and semi-desert terrain. Since they expected to be hanged, "they often broke down in tears and confessed in torrents of detail when informed they would probably only serve a prison term—unless they had killed."[9]

In 1963, Rhodesia amended her Law and Order Act to require sentence of death for anyone who entered the country with weapons of war. Vigorous enforcement of this measure virtually ended the fire-bombings of African villages and the murder of African Chiefs by ZANU and ZAPU thugs. With the restoration of order, the law was amended to provide that judges should determine whether persons guilty under the act should be imprisoned or hanged in accordance with the evidence. Thus, in 1968, Rhodesian terrorists were given long terms of imprisonment and only those guilty of murder were hanged. Even this aroused the wrath of Prime Minister Wilson, who considered these executions sufficient reason for him to break off negotiations with Rhodesia in March 1968.[10] Under Rhodesia's security legislation, the place and condi-

[9]*Ibid.*, p. 11.
[10]"Rhodesia: New Talks Fail," *Bulletin of the Afrika Instituut*, Pretoria, Vol. II, No. 1 (January–February 1969), pp. 9–10.

tions of imprisonment of terrorists and infiltrators cannot be disclosed. Despite the savage murders and tortures perpetrated by Communist terrorists in Angola and Mozambique, Portugal has refrained from imposing the death penalty, which was abolished in 1810.

On the Rhodesian front, counter-insurgency operations are the responsibility of the British South African Police (B.S.A.P.), an organization which dates from the days of Cecil Rhodes, and the Rhodesian African Rifles, a force composed of Black troops and White officers. One of their main functions has been to render the African "Ho Chi Minh Trail," a 400-mile-long supply route along the Mozambique-Rhodesian frontier, unusable to the enemy.

In their actions against Rhodesia, the terrorists have suffered from their lack of any solid base of support in the African population. The tribal Chiefs and Headmen remember the years of terror, in which the ZAPU and ZANU forces spread murder and arson among the Black people of Rhodesia. Because of this and because of the harmony between the tribal Africans and the Rhodesian Government, infiltrators are very often handed over to the authorities by the Natives and there is no evidence of disloyalty among the ranks of the Rhodesian African Rifles or the B.S.A.P.[11]

South Africa cooperates with Rhodesia, Portuguese Angola and Mozambique in the eradication of the scourge of terrorism. Prime Minister Vorster stated in 1968 that, while South Africa has no defense agreement with either country, "we are good friends and good friends do not need an agreement to combat murderers. Good friends

[11]Ministry of Information, Immigration and Tourism, Government of Rhodesia, *Jackal Hunt One*. Salisbury, 1968, 7 pp. This article is a reprint from *Outpost*, organ of the B.S.A.P., for March 1968.

know what their duty is when their neighbor's house is on fire. . . . We shall act in any country where we are asked to act by the government of that country."

In August 1968, the South African Defense Force held "Exercise Sibasa," in which 5,000 troops were deployed to repel and destroy a terrorist invasion in the heavily wooded areas of Northeastern Transvaal. The exercise was characterized by South African Defense Minister Botha as the most important attempted since World War II. Lieutenant General C. A. Fraser, who commanded the operation, held meetings with the Chiefs of the Venda and Tsonga people who inhabit the area so that tribal customs and taboos would not be upset and the presence of the troops would not be resented. Paramount Chief Mpephu of the Vendas announced that they would "defend the country with their kierries" in case of terrorist attack. He instructed all Headmen and all women and children to be on the lookout for infiltrators and report their presence. The Paramount Chief considered the Red Chinese the Vendas' worst enemy, as the Chinese who had been brought into South Africa in 1910 had, he believed, "devoured African children."[12]

The policy of the South African Government, one that is backed by the opposition United Party, is to fight terrorist attacks on any and all peaceful neighboring countries when it is invited to do so, and to strike at terrorists, who are using neighboring countries as an access route to South Africa, wherever they can be hit. On this basis, South Africa has placed a force of about 300 police in Rhodesia to help the Rhodesian Rifles and the B.S.A.P. Some of these South Africans had been wounded by late 1968 and at least one had been killed. A central counter-

[12]*The Friend* (an opposition daily newspaper), August 22, 1968.

insurgency command for the forces of the three countries under attack has been set up, and an efficient system of radio communication ensures that information is routed promptly to wherever it is needed so that manpower, matériel and supplies can be swiftly concentrated in any country or region threatened by attack.

The Assault on Mozambique

No sooner had the rebellion in Angola been reduced to intermittent guerrilla warfare than similar trouble broke out in Mozambique. FRELIMO, the *Frente Libertação Moçambique*,[13] a Communist organization, was being virtually torn apart in 1963 because of the struggle for power within its ranks of two ambitious leaders, Adelino Gwambe and Uria Simango. At this point, Dr. Eduardo Mondlane was summoned from his post as Professor of African Studies in Syracuse University to Dar es Salaam to head and reunify the organization.

Mondlane's background is interesting. During the Kennedy Administration, he had been used to train American volunteers for the Peace Corps destined for Malawi, a territory bordering on Mozambique. Since Mondlane's connection with FRELIMO was notorious at the time, his appointment seemed inconsistent with the supposedly non-political character of the Peace Corps. The fact that Portugal was a NATO ally did not prevent President Kennedy's people from appointing a professional revolutionary whose avowed aim was to levy war against that country.

After acquiring a White American coed wife, Mondlane toured East European countries in search of arms for FRELIMO and then set up headquarters in Dar es Salaam,

[13]Front for the Liberation of Mozambique.

a focal center of the Communist push into White Africa. In 1964, the year in which he proclaimed Mozambique would be "liberated," Mondlane got substantial supplies of arms, allegedly of Chinese Communist origin. However, Mondlane's FRELIMO was the political arm of Soviet Communism in Mozambique, as opposed to COREMO, which was a Chinese Communist instrumentality. Mondlane's wife claimed that the movement received American financial support through the Mozambique Institute, which had close Ford Foundation connections.

When Mondlane took over the leadership of FRELIMO, Lucas Fernández, another ambitious Negro politician, left the organization and founded the more activist MANU.[14] Picking up weapons and ammunition from Soviet sources, he recruited a gang of terrorists, slipped across the Mozambique border at night and struck the first blow of the war of "liberation." At a place called Vila Cabral, he called a mass meeting of tribesmen, at which he shot Father Daniel, an aged priest and medical missionary, in the back and then inflicted 33 stab wounds on the dying man. Boasting that he had "killed a white man," Fernández fled across the border, but was subsequently captured and placed in a Mozambique prison camp with 2,000 other terrorists. An incurable schizophrenic, Fernández today denies that he killed Father Daniel and attributes the deed to a wholly mythical alter ego.[15]

On September 25, 1964, Mondlane's FRELIMO forces raided into Mozambique from Tanzania. Large areas of northern Mozambique fell prey to the ambushes, hit-and-run raids and assassinations of the terrorists. By 1966, Portugal was obliged to have 45,000 troops garrisoned in

[14]Mozambique African National Union.
[15]For details, v. Brigham, *op. cit.*, pp. 22–25.

Angola and another 25,000 in Mozambique. By early 1969, the Portuguese possessions in Africa were being defended by 100,000 troops.

Despite the fact that Portugal is one of the poorest countries in Europe, she spent 6.7 per cent of her 1968 gross national product on the war against terrorism in Africa, whereas South Africa, the ultimate target of the insurrectionaries, spent only 1.1 per cent of her gross national product on defense.

South Africa has indicated that she will support the Portuguese military effort financially and with manpower and matériel whenever that becomes necessary. "South Africa has an interest in what happens in Angola and Mozambique," Defense Minister Botha declared in 1968. ". . . The onslaughts there are aimed at the Republic in the final instance. About that we can have no illusions." If the terrorist offensive gained in momentum, he added, "it will be a case of not only Portuguese soldiers fighting, but our own young men, who will then withdraw from the economic sphere to form a phalanx on our northern borders." In September 1968, Sir de Villiers Graaff, leader of the opposition United Party in South Africa, called for stepped-up non-military aid to the Portuguese counter-insurgency effort in Angola and Mozambique.

The Stakes in Portuguese Africa

One of the major stakes in the struggle is the gigantic hydroelectric project to dam the Zambesi River at Cabora Bassa in Mozambique and provide more power than that yielded by the Aswan Dam. South Africa has agreed to take the entire surplus power output from Cabora Bassa, thus obtaining one of the cheapest electric power sources in the world. Zamco, the international consortium of the

Oppenheimer-controlled Anglo-American Corporation, has been awarded the contract to complete the first phase of the project at an estimated cost of $230 million. Thus, both capital investment and purchase of the power produced will be primarily South African.

What Portugal expects to gain from the project is the irrigation of 3.7 million acres for agriculture on which an estimated one million Portuguese immigrants are to be settled, thereby transforming Mozambique demographically, providing an impregnable bulwark against invasion and relieving overpopulation and land shortage in Portugal itself. In addition, cheap power will make it possible for Mozambique to exploit an estimated 60 million tons of rich iron ore, a 12-mile seam of coking coal together with resources of such minerals and ores as manganese, copper, nickel, fluorspar, chrome, asbestos and titaniferous magnetites.

Cabora Bassa, however, lies close to the Tanzanian frontier and the terrorists are determined to destroy the project by sabotage. The PIDE (*Policia Internacionale de Defense do Estado*)[16] has taken effective counter measures, such as advancing its operational headquarters into the northern area and constricting the FRELIMO-harassed area to about half its maximum size of 4,000 square miles. Captured guerrilla fighters and infiltrators are rehabilitated where possible and sent back to their tribal areas to detect and repulse raiding parties. Since these men are regarded with suspicion by their fellow tribesmen and are likely to be killed by them if they seem about to return to the Communist camp, they are under a strong inducement to remain loyal to the regime. As of October 1968, none had become a renegade.[17]

[16]International Police for the Defense of the State.
[17]Brigham, *op. cit.*, p. 29.

The Kunene hydroelectric project on the border between South West Africa and Angola is a similar cooperative venture, which is also exposed to terrorist raids and sabotage. Kunene is to harness the energy of the Raucana Falls at an estimated capital cost of $610 million, irrigating 1.2 million acres at present untilled and providing land on which half a million Portuguese peasants can be settled. It is also vital to the development of Ovamboland in the north of South West Africa. Perhaps even more important is a projected Portuguese–South African consortium to exploit the immensely rich oil reserves of Portuguese Angola and Cabinda.[18]

The Terrorists and their Friends

Whatever successes the Communist instigators of terror achieved were in part due to their endorsement by liberal-to-leftist American politicians and intellectuals who sought to palm them off on a badly informed public as crusaders for justice and freedom. These American friends of the African terror included the incurably naive patsies who fall for every plausible leftwing cause, windbags, politicians ready to sacrifice their country's interests in return for the Negro vote, and intellectuals who became fellow travellers of Black Power because it seemed to them the "in" thing to do. Others were motivated by resentments of obscure pathological origin and by self-hatred turned outward toward the ethnic group, civilization and class to which they themselves belonged.

One of the most consistent mouthpieces for the African terrorists was Hubert Horatio Humphrey. Humphrey defended Antoine Gizenga and Christophe Gbenye, the

[18]South Africa lacks oil fields. The 1970 production target for Cabinda oil was recently raised from 2 to 7.5 million tons.

Communist or pro-Communist Vice Premier and police chief of the Congo respectively, on the Senate floor in September 1961. He assured Americans that the Algerian National Liberation Front was "basically friendly" to the United States. The front, when it came to power, promptly ushered in a Communist revolution, transformed Algeria into a Soviet client state and made the great naval base at Mers el Kébir available to the Soviet Mediterranean Fleet. As might have been expected, Humphrey served as an American apologist for Holden Roberto, who was responsible for the gruesome butcheries of Angola settlers and their wives and children, described in a previous chapter.

Together with such luminaries as Arthur Schlesinger, Jr., the late Bishop James Pike and Norman Thomas,[19] Humphrey sponsored the American Committee on Africa. This organization "openly supports terrorists and Communists" who oppose South Africa, Rhodesia and Portugal and it indulged in an ingenious defense of Braam Fischer. As late as 1962, Humphrey stated in writing that the American Committee "used my name on its letterhead with my full knowledge and consent" and added that it was "a reputable organization pursuing a worthwhile cause."[20]

In 1968, when he was Vice President of the United States, Humphrey made a state visit to Zambia and Ethiopia. In the former country, he allowed himself to be accompanied by American Negro Communists who would emerge later in that same year as "officials" of the so-

[19]Norman Thomas, the perennial leader of the American Socialist Party, was a man of honor and integrity. However, he was approaching eighty in 1962; his mental powers were declining, and he was frequently deluded into serving as the front for evil causes.
[20]Allan H. Ryskind, *Hubert*. New Rochelle: Arlington House, 1968, pp. 307–09.

called Republic of New Africa. The avowed purpose of this "republic" was the treasonable one of wresting Louisiana, Mississippi, Alabama, South Carolina and western Georgia from the United States by revolutionary means. Humphrey also reviewed terrorist armed bands in two Zambia training camps and declared at a state dinner: "America is on the side of the Black countries (of Africa) in their fight against the White South."[21] This statement was broadcast on the Chinese Communist radio at Dar es Salaam and spread throughout Black Africa by Communist agents of both the Chinese and the Soviet brand as providing proof that "the second biggest man, the Vice President of the most powerful nation—Black or White—in the world" supported the Red campaign of terror and proletarian revolution.[22]

Six weeks before his departure on this catastrophic tour, Humphrey was urged to exercise extreme caution in his public statements by American diplomatic officials in East Africa. Either this advice never reached the Vice President or he chose to ignore it. Since it can be assumed that Humphrey was adequately briefed at some time prior to his African jaunt, it appears probable that he decided to follow Lear's advice to Edgar and Gloucester:

> . . . Get thee glass eyes;
> And, like a scurvy politician, seem
> To see the things thou dost not.[23]

Mondlane's End

Eduardo Mondlane lived in ease and luxury in the safety of Dar es Salaam, while his FRELIMO followers infiltrated

[21]Brigham, *op cit.*, pp. 18–19.
[22]*Idem.*
[23]Act IV, Scene 6.

across the Mozambique border and took all the risks. This occasioned a good deal of resentment among the rank and file and among the more hotheaded elements.[24]

A "moderate" terrorist, Dr. Mondlane opposed all-out invasion of Mozambique as suicidal. His ideal was to "work like the Vietcong." The fact that he was intelligent, had been a professor in an American university and had a White wife made FRELIMO seem respectable and opened financial and political doors that would otherwise have been firmly shut.

In early February of 1969, Dr. Eduardo Mondlane, who had been responsible for so much slaughter in Mozambique, was killed by a bomb, planted by unknown hands. If his death was engineered by the Portuguese, then the fact that the leader of FRELIMO was not even safe in his Dar es Salaam headquarters may well have made some of his followers pause for thought. If it was the work of rival terrorist politicians, it merely stressed the extent to which the movement was poisoned by personal ambitions and factional strife. The liquidation of Mondlane removed a skillful and intelligent leader. If tactical extremists should seize contral of FRELIMO and attempt to realize their absurd dream of a march on Lourenço Marques, the capital of Mozambique, the Bloemfontein *Volksblad* of February 4, 1969, speculated, "one can only hope that in a large-scale confrontation the Portuguese forces will dispose of this rodent peril to their country once and for all."

Despite the fact that Portugal was one of America's NATO allies, the Nixon Administration, through State Department Press Officer Robert McCloskey, made this extraordinary statement: "Mr. Mondlane was a well-known and respected figure, both in Africa and in the

[24]*Die Volksblad*, Bloemfontein daily. Editorial of February 4, 1969.

United States. The Department of State regrets his assassination, which we believe can only be viewed as a brutal and senseless act of violence."[25]

To term the assassination of a leader who lived by violence and terror "senseless" seemed the height of fatuousness. Since the Nixon Administration had held office a mere fortnight, it was not necessary to infer that the old Kennedy-Johnson policy of fawning on African terrorists, armed and controlled by America's Communist enemies, was in full force. It seemed equally possible that the inept McCloskey was an ephemeral phenomenon.

The Terrorists Retreat

In January 1969, Lieutenant General C. A. Fraser, the officer in command of Joint South African Combat Forces, visited operational areas in Mozambique and reported that he was "tremendously impressed by the way they are carrying on this job of counter-insurgency both in the fields of military and of civil administration, and by the success they are having." This marked a new stage in General Staff consultations and military cooperation between the two countries and coincided in time with the summit meeting in Khartoum, under the auspices of the Organization of African Unity, of all the terrorist parties operating against White Africa.

Some of the Black African states were beginning to close their borders to the terrorists. Botswana (formerly Bechuanaland) imprisoned 34 Zambian terrorists in September 1967 and, at the beginning of 1968, doubled its security forces. Malawi, under its able President, Dr. Hastings Banda, is a recipient of South African economic aid for

[25]State Department Press Briefing, February 4, 1969.

development and is inhospitable to terrorists. Similarly, Lesotho (formerly Basutoland) and Swaziland cooperate economically with South Africa and refuse to take part in the OAU program of invasion and racial war. The Malagasy Republic (formerly Madagascar) is under an outspokenly anti-Communist leader, President Philibert Tsiranana, and is not involved in the conspiracies hatched in Zambia, Tanzania and Ethiopia.

Even the Zambian policy is not unequivocal. The series of terrorist setbacks, the development of a strong tripartite counter-insurgency system and the eruption of violent conflict, sometimes armed, among the various terrorist factions led President Kaunda to have a chain of so-called Freedom Houses, which served as command posts for terrorist operations, closed down in the fall of 1968. Whether this order was a move to deny terrorists freedom of action in Zambia or a move to make them fight on pain of expulsion remained unclear. Vice President Kapwepwe of Zambia, a Maoist Communist, has openly challenged Kaunda's leadership in boastful speeches to the training camps. The Zambian regular army with British–trained officers serves as a counter-force to Kapwepwe and has mauled the terrorist bands whenever it was given an opportunity to do so.[26] President Kaunda has also taken action to eliminate the Red press gangs, which kidnap Zambians for service in the terrorist units. He complained that Zambians "who did not want such service were so severely beaten that many died."

In an effort to acquire the modern arms necessary for an invasion of White Africa, Vice President Kapwepwe went to France in December 1967 to get Fouga Magister jets and Alouette helicopters, but the French demanded

[26]Brigham, *op. cit.*, pp. 32–33.

cash on the line. The following summer, President Kaunda went to London to obtain Rapier supersonic missiles on credit, but received the same answer and the additional comment that the Zambians were incapable of handling such sophisticated weaponry.

One of the reasons for Zambia's desire for these offensive weapons is the ever-present fear that South African, Rhodesian or Portuguese forces may launch raids against the guerrilla training camps and totally destroy them. This is well within the military capabilities of the counter-insurgency forces and there is a good deal of speculation as to why it has not been done. While lacking any specific knowledge of motives, I should like to suggest three considerations that may have prevented offensive action of this sort.

First, destruction of the training camps might have served as a pretext for massive Soviet and Chinese escalation of the struggle, probably taking the form of accelerated influx of military forces and supplies and possibly *coups d'etat* to put outright Communist regimes in control of such invasion staging areas as Zambia and Tanzania. As long as the Kennedy and Johnson Administrations were in office, no positive American reaction to that threat could have been anticipated. It was even possible that the elements that had spawned the Carnegie Endowment master plan for the invasion and conquest of South Africa might have succeeded in committing Washington to work through the United Nations to engineer a joint Soviet-American blow against White Africa.

A second possible consideration was that, since the guerrilla movement was already being disintegrated by counter-insurgency, raids on the training camps, which might arouse a defensive and nationalist reaction, should be avoided.

A third factor may have been the conviction that the era of Democrat rule in the United States and of Labour Government in Britain was coming to an end. If so, any blow against the training camps should be postponed until new regimes, more alive to the national interests of their countries, took office.

South African Defense

During the Kennedy-Johnson era, the United States consistently refused to sell Portugal the arms she needed to protect her African citizens. Consequently, Portuguese aviators flew obsolescent planes, which were often poorly maintained, and Portuguese infantrymen went into the bush on search-and-destroy missions with weapons that were far from up to date, thus unnecessarily increasing their casualties.

As long as America's African policy was dominated by people of the mentality of Vice President Humphrey, a total denial of arms sales to South Africa applied. With British arms also denied her, South Africa turned to France and simultaneously began to develop a powerful armaments industry of her own.

Between 1960/61 and 1964/65, South Africa increased her expenditure on munitions manufacture 100-fold, and by the latter year, 120 licenses to manufacture weapons had been issued; the Republic was, according to Minister of Defense Fouché, "practically self-sufficient so far as the production of small weapons, ammunition and explosives were concerned." As early as August 1965, South Africa, with the largest uranium resources on earth, inaugurated her first nuclear reactor, Safari I.[27]

[27]Safari does not refer to big game hunting, but stands for South African Fundamental Atomic Research Installation.

In late 1968, Minister of Defense Botha announced that a Decca radar screen was being built to give South Africa an early warning system reaching 200 miles out to sea. It was self-evident that the radar system would be worthless without surface-to-air (SAM) missiles. However, in 1965, the British Labour Government turned down a $170 million South African order for Bloodhound missiles to serve this purpose. As early as 1963, South Africa tackled the problem of producing her own short- and intermediate-range rockets. These were apparently in production by 1968, and in the fall of that year, South Africa opened her first missile range for experimental launchings on the Zululand coast. Unfortunately, the 30-by-10-mile site chosen includes St. Lucia Lake, which is not only the world's largest salt water estuary, but a magnificent wild life preserve, rich is hippopotamuses, rhinos and crocodiles.

By the end of 1968, South Africa was also producing armored cars and her own jet trainers.[28] An expansion of shipbuilding facilities and the creation of ARMSCOR, a $140-million state-owned armaments combine, emphasized the fact that South Africa was not only defending her land frontiers against guerrillas, but was moving with giant strides into the power vacuum created in the Indian Ocean when Britain scuttled her Empire, lost her will to rule and reneged on her international commitments.

Although it was inspired by malevolence, the Kennedy-Johnson and Macmillan-Wilson crusade against White Africa has had the opposite of its intended effect. It has

[28]The Labour Government refused to permit shipment of aircraft to South Africa. When the Hawker-Siddeley airplane factory laid off 1,2000 skilled workers, the Lord Mayor of Portsmouth complained that "if we were allowed to supply South Africa with Buccaneers we would have been alright." Many of the dismissed workers were recruited for the $40 million Atlas Aircraft Corporation plant near Johannesburg, which went on stream in late 1967 and is producing Impala jet trainers.

solidified the nationalism and sense of unity of the beleaguered populations and has inspired them to efforts that in normal times might have proved impossible. Partly as a result, South Africa is emerging toward the status of a world power, is producing the weapons needed for her own defense and that of the Cape route, and is developing vast economic complexes in the guerrilla-menaced areas of Mozambique and Angola. Rhodesia is striding toward total independence and Portuguese Africa is planning White settlement on such a massive scale as to render successful invasion from the North impossible. At the moment of writing, the forces of terror and chaos feel beaten and are in disarray. There is a renewed hope that South Africa may soon be able to devote her enormous creative energies to the peaceful development and modernization of her own country and to the assistance of those Black republics willing to live with her as good neighbors.

The United States has an opportunity to reverse the vindictive and mean policies of the past and to cooperate with South Africa, Rhodesia, Portugal, the Malagasy Republic, Botswana, Lesotho and Malawi in an experiment in peaceful coexistence between White and Black states, based on common interests, peace, due process of law, individual freedom and cooperation in economic and social development.

Index